CLASS ACTS

OTHER BOOKS BY MARY MITCHELL:

Dear Ms.Demeanor: The Young Person's Etiquette Guide

The Complete Idiot's Guide to Etiquette

*The First Five Minutes: How to Make a Great First Impression
in Any Business Situation*

The Complete Idiot's Guide to Business Etiquette

Copyright © 2002 by Mary Mitchell

M. Evans and Company, Inc.
216 East 49th Street
New York, New York 10017

Library of Congress Cataloging-in-Publication Data

Mitchell, Mary, 1949–
    Class acts : how good manners create good relationships and good rela-
tionships create good business / Mary Mitchell
    p. cm.
    ISBN 0-87131-979-9
    1. Business etiquette. 2. Interpersonal communication. 3. Organizational
behavior. 4. Communication in organizations. I. Title.
HF5389 .M577 2002
650.1'3—dc21   2002192511

Book design by Terry Bain

Printed in the United States of America

9   8   7   6   5   4   3   2   1

CLASS ACTS

How Good Manners Create
Good Relationships and
Good Relationships Create
Good Business

Mary Mitchell

M. EVANS AND COMPANY, INC.
New York

I am delighted to dedicate this book to my honorary children,
Janel Dixon, Carolyn Ferko, Daniel Rudasill, and Eileen Weinstein.
Each of you is a Class Act.

Contents

Foreword	xvii
Author's Preface	xix
Acknowledgements	xxi
Introduction	xxiii

Part I: What is a Class Act

Chapter 1: The Constants, from Children to CEOs 3
    What Is a Class Act to Mary Mitchell? 3
    Remaining a Class Act, Even Through Crises 4
    What Is a Class Act to Others? 5

Chapter 2: A Class Act Has Self Confidence 7
    Confidence 7
    Movement 8
    Attire and Grooming 8
    Breathing 9
    Self-Discipline 9
    Giving and Receiving 10

Chapter 3: A Class Act Exemplifies the Virtues
of Accountability and Forgiveness 11
    Meet a Bullying Boss 13
    Forgiveness Defined 14
    The Mechanics of Forgiveness 14
    Responsibility 15

Chapter 4: A Class Act Exemplifies the Virtue of Trustworthiness 17
    Secrets, Sacred Secrets 17
    Gossip: Second-Hand Poison 18
    What Makes Stand-up People Stand Out 19
    Gossip 19
    Stop the Gossip 20

Chapter 5: Why a Corporation Must Also Be a Class Act 22
    What is Corporate Governance? 23
    The Constituencies (Read "People") 23
    Conclusion 25

Chapter 6: A Class Act Is Never Rude   27
How Rudeness Really Affects Business   29
The Ten Most Common Business Mistakes to Avoid   29

Part II: Learn a Necessary Skill

Chapter 7: A Class Act Requires Peace   37
Tuning Out to Tune In - Unplugging   37
Meditation   37
The Relaxation Response   38
Definition of Terms   39
A Simple Stress Test   40
Personal Preferences in Practice   40

Chapter 8: Einstein Had the Answer   43
Answers in the Form of a Prayer   44

Part III: Communicating

Chapter 9: A Class Act Communicates Well   49
Perception   50
Get Off to a Good Start   50
The Basics of Communicating   51
Body Language   51
The Art of Listening   51
Ten Listening Skills   52
Giving Negative Feedback in a Positive Way   53

Chapter 10: Introductions by a Class Act   55
Meetings and Greetings—The Mechanics   55
Time to Speak   57
Handling Miserable Moments   58
Remembering Names   59
Twelve Ways to Sabotage Yourself   60

Chapter 11: A Class Act Makes Conversation   61
First Impressions   61
Making Small Talk   63
Become a Good Listener   63
Here Are Some Ways to Get a Conversation Going   64
The Anatomy of a Conversationalist   65

Handling Miserable Moments   66
A Class Act Never Asks These Questions   67

Chapter 12: A Class Act Knows How to
Disagree Without Being Disagreeable   69
Always Disagree in Private, if Possible   70
Don't Let Your Tone of Voice Betray You   70
Fair-Fighting Tips   71
A Class Act Will Practice These Principles   73

Chapter 13: A Class Act Knows How to Use All Telephones   75
Class Acts Know and Use Telephone Basics   75
Cell Phones   80
Teleconferencing   82
A Class Act Practices Telephone Etiquette   84

Chapter 14: A Class Act Retains Humanity in Cyberspace   85
CyberChallenges: E-Mail and the Internet   85
Netiquette Rules   86
Addressing   86
Formatting   86
Flaming   87
Hoaxes   88
Spam   88
Security   88
Passwords   88
Copyright   89
Web Surfing   89

Chapter 15: A Class Act Knows the Power of Handwritten Notes   91
The Pen Is Mightier Than the Palm   91
A Well-Written Letter Has Magical Powers   92
A Return to the Old-Fashioned   92
Stationery "Wardrobes"   93
Some Writing Advice   94

Chapter 16: A Class Act Has No Fear of Public Speaking   95
Fear of Public Speaking Is Quite Common   95
The Physiology of Stage Fright   96
Meditation and Visualization   96
As a Member of the Audience   97

Part IV: Life Skills (On and Off the Job)

Chapter 17: A Class Act Is Healthy in Body and Mind 101

Honor Yourself 101
Self-Respect and Maintenance 102
Working Out and Sportsmanship 104
Exercise Pathway Etiquette 105
Exercise Class Etiquette 106
Locker-Room Diplomacy 107

Chapter 18: A Class Act Knows What to Wear and How to Wear It 108

Fashion Judgments 109
Clothes—The Mechanics 109
Quality Through and Through 111
Choosing What to Wear 111
Basic Wardrobe Buying Guidelines—Women 112
Men's Basic Wardrobe 113
Business Casual 113
Summer Style at Work 114
Tips for Professional-Looking Hair 117

Chapter 19: A Class Act Is Generous of Spirit—Gifts and Contributions 120

Giving Gifts and Making Contributions 120
Time and Attention 121
To Tithe Is a Personal and Private Choice 121
Office Gifts: The Rules 122
E-Gifts 122
Recycling Gifts 123
Always Add a Personal Touch 123
Ten Key Questions 124
Stuck for Gift Ideas? 124

Chapter 20: A Class Act Knows the Difference Between Service and Servitude—Appropriate Tipping in the Business Environment 126

A Life Lesson 126
Be a Generous Tipper 127
Part of Your Team 127
General Tipping Guidelines 128
Salons, Personal Service 130
Remember the Holidays 130

Part V: Office Opportunities and Minefields

Chapter 21: A Class Act Is a Model of Consistency,
Compassion, and Civility 135
A Class Act Lives by the Rules of Etiquette in Business 136
Keeping the Boss Happy 138
Asking for a Raise 139
Refocus Your Priorities 139

Chapter 22: A Class Act Knows How to
Conduct Meetings with Skill 141
Open Your Mind 141
Round Up the Usual Suspects 142
The Five Ps 143
Learn from the Best 144
When Attending Meetings, Remember To: 145
Whether Chairing or Attending a Meeting, Always . . . 146

Chapter 23: A Class Act Doesn't Mix Romance with Work 147
A Corporate Policy on Dating 147
Don't Flaunt Your Relationship 148
Think Before You Ask a Co-worker or Client for a Date 149
Superiors Dating Subordinates 150
What If All Goes Well . . . 150
The Big Picture, In Brief 151
What Not to Do 151
And If You Do Get Caught Red-Faced . . . 153

Chapter 24: When a Class Act Works Successfully from Home 154
The Ups and Downs of Working from Home 154
The Branch Office—Your Car 158
Establish Rituals 159

Part VI: Food and Drink

Chapter 25: A Class Act at Table 163
The Etiquette of Dining 163
Further Dining-Table Guidelines That Always Apply 166
A Class Act's Demeanor at Table 167
How a Class Act Handles Tricky Foods 168

Chapter 26: A Class Act at The Formal Meal, Buffet, Banquet   171

    The Formal Meal   171

    The Wine Service   173

    The Courses   174

    Afternoon Tea and High Tea   175

    Braving the Buffet—Don't Be Baffled   176

Chapter 27: A Class Act at Cocktail Parties and Receptions   179

    Remember: Business Is Business   180

    The Mechanics of Being a Good Guest   180

    Circulate, Circulate, Circulate!   182

    The Mechanics for the Host   182

Chapter 28: A Class Act Hosts Restaurant Meals Confidently   184

    The Business Meal   184

    It All Comes Down to Manners   185

    You Need to Be in Control   186

    The Class Act as Host   187

    Anatomy of a Restaurant   188

Chapter 29: A Class Act Isn't Intimidated by Wine   190

    Choosing a Wine   190

    Approving the Wine   191

    At Home   192

    There's Always More to Learn   192

Chapter 30: A Class Act Knows How

(and When) to Drink with Colleagues   193

    It Seems So Simple, But . . .   193

    No One Ever *Has* to Drink   194

    Stick to the Two-Drink Limit   194

    Be Yourself   194

    Use Your Head   195

Part VII: The Class Act Is a Gracious Host

Chapter 31: A Class Act Entertains at Home   199

    The Best Place to Do Business   199

    Start With a Small Soiree   200

    The Guest List   202

    Seating Logic   203

Ways to Head Off Potential Disaster with CLASS 204

The Rules of Reciprocity 205

Chapter 32: The Class Act Entertains in Restaurants 206

The Importance of the Venue 206

Choosing a Restaurant 206

Issuing Invitations 207

Dress Rehearsal 207

Your Role as Host 208

Subtly Control the Seating Order 208

Ordering Drinks 208

Ordering Dinner 209

Selecting the Wine 209

When to Talk Business, and Dessert 210

Paying, Tipping, and Leaving 210

Chapter 33: A Class Act Entertains at a Private Club 212

The Etiquette of Clubs 212

Social Club 212

Private Club 213

At Your Boss's Club 214

Part VIII: The Circle of Life

Chapter 34: A Class Act Celebrates the Passages of Life 217

Gifts vs. Cards 218

Engagements 219

Bridal Showers 219

Weddings 219

Births 220

Christenings, Bar Mitzvahs, and Bat Mitzvahs 220

Birthdays 220

Retirement 220

Chapter 35: A Class Act Understands the Etiquette of Condolence 222

Both of Us Were in the Wrong 223

A Cold-Hearted Rationalizer 223

What to Say and How to Say It 224

Part IX: Difficult Conversations and Faux Pas Rescues

Chapter 36: A Class Act Understands Tough Love   231

    Delivering Bad News   231

    Firing Someone   232

    Handling Other Uncomfortable Situations   233

    Handling More Serious Issues   236

Chapter 37: A Class Act Knows How to Use the Word "No"   239

    Easier with the Family   239

    The Principles of Saying "No"   240

    The Rules of Non-Engagement   240

    The Rules for Saying "No" at Work   241

Chapter 38: A Class Act Understands Cosmetic Procedures   243

    As the Crow's Feet Fly   243

    A Delayed Reaction   243

    Some Do's And Don'ts   244

Part X: Doing the Right Thing

Chapter 39: A Class Act Knows How to Apologize Well   249

    Own Up to the Truth   249

    The Mechanics of Apology   250

Chapter 40: Epilogue: A Civil, Successful and Centered Man   253

    First Impressions Aside . . .   253

    A Retired Corporate Lawyer, Clarence Pays Attention   254

    An Infectious Laugh and Compassionate Heart   254

    A Man of Action   255

    An Inspiration   255

Appendix A: A Class Act and Meditation   257

    The Sacred Gift   257

    The "Five I's" Are   258

    Human Being vs. Human Doing   258

    The Process   258

    Physical Changes by an Unwilling Yogi   260

    Experiment with Your Own Meditation Process   261

    The Text to Relax Your Body and Mind   261

The Countdown   263
Visiting My Health Level: The Fab Five   264
Now I Gratefully Visit My Career Level   264
Now I Celebrate Relationships   265
The Wrap-Up   266
Voilà!   266

Index   267
About the Author   276

Foreword

Class Acts is the important new look at business and corporate manners for this century.

And I can say this, as the first published author on business manners, back in the 1970s, when the world was so different: Mary Mitchell's solid approach is based on accountability and integrity.

I have been Mary's proud mentor for some years. She builds on my earlier reference works with a "how to" for the entire workplace audience—providing the best advice, the best understanding, and the clearest prose, so they will comprehend, utilize, and become Class Acts.

Read, study, enjoy, and prosper!

Letitia Baldrige
Washington, D.C.
October 2002

Author's Preface

People ask me all the time if I agree with them that the world is becoming ruder by the minute. Yes, I do. When I ask myself why this is so, I have only to look at the miracles of technology for the answer.

Then I stop and realize that the miracles of technology merely provide the many opportunities for expanding rudeness. The cause is more discreet. . . . Is it not the growing greed and acquisitiveness that pervades our society that is in fact the causal force?

It appears to me that we have traded our compassion, kindness, consideration, and, in many ways, our very integrity so that we may utilize the new technology and its attendant means to acquire more money and power.

I was struck by a full-page ad in *The New York Times* that boasted, "Never be bored in a meeting again." It went on to say that if you purchased this new whiz-bang gizmo, you could do your holiday shopping, purchase theater tickets, order dinner, plan your vacation, check your stock portfolio, and answer your e-mail—all while you are being paid to focus on the meeting agenda. That's rude. It's crazy. It's one example of why we're all running on tilt.

The breakdown of human interaction—phone responses converted to endless menus, an obsession for immediate gratification, financial and otherwise—allows the new technology to support, indeed foster, systemic rudeness.

Remember when stores were closed on Sundays? Remember when commuters said that, annoying as a thirty-minute ride to work might be, the time provided an opportunity to decompress, to regroup, to reflect? Now there is no escape from the cell phone, whether in your car or on the train or bus. There's just no down time and no time for the solutions that come to us during such meditative periods.

I am all for the miraculous technology I seem to berate. But, let's utilize it with *manners*. We must remember that for each and every action, there will be an equal and opposite reaction. We just need to allow time in our thinking and behavior to compensate and regain our civility.

Mary Mitchell
Philadelphia, Pa.

Acknowledgments

Reflecting on the Class Acts who helped make this book possible makes me both humble and profoundly grateful.

In particular, John C. Pine, the worldly wordsmith who helped shape both my thinking and the manuscript itself. Clarence Vandegrift's stubbornly linear mind saw me through the frustrating and tedious edits demanded by PJ Dempsey, who is by far the most gifted (and tenacious) editor with whom I've ever had the privilege of working. Nancy Love, a wise agent indeed, gets credit for our author/editor dynamic duo.

Robin Eaton's illustrations give the book energy and whimsy that my words could not do by themselves.

I relied on the skills and coaching of Barry Eisen and John Felitto to keep me centered. Following Michael Losier's advice helped me attract all the right support from all the right people. Susan Farrell managed impeccably to organize a roomful of random notes into files according to the table of contents—a daunting task at best. And Elizabeth Humphries patiently, carefully, and lovingly transcribed my meditation tape, which appears in the Appendix. Dan Rudasill, my cyberhero and technical guru, and Barbara Williams, my indispensable virtual assistant, never let myriad calls for help go unanswered.

Jack Bittler, Betsy Salunek, Gail Zales, and Jane Dalton really "got it" that *Class Acts* was more than simply another etiquette book to me, and never failed to support me in doing my best to make the world a kinder place.

Letitia Baldrige taught me all the etiquette I know, from the time I was a teenager devouring her books. What an astounding privilege to have had the benefit of her time, attention, wisdom, and, most of all, her example.

Thea Lammers Long continues to be my idea of the consummate communicator, and I am indebted and grateful to be her student.

Robert, Julia, and Shane Brackup, my awesomely lovable nephews and niece, kept me in touch with what's important in life and, without knowing it, were great teachers.

Dan Fleischmann, my husband and very best friend, never once complained about the disadvantages of being married to an author who gets up in the middle of the night to write. In fact, he makes me believe that such quirks are part of my charm. More than anyone in the world, he is the wind beneath my wings.

Were it not for Sheila Cluff and the remarkable individuals who frequent and teach at The Oaks at Ojai, California, I never would have learned yoga and self-hypnosis. Those practices have added invaluable dimensions to my life and contributions to this book.

Finally, I hope the following Class Acts will accept my gratitude for giving me so much support during the process of writing this book, as well as for sharing their own thoughts of what a class act is:

Mary Chollet, Maureen Carmen, John Corr, Jacquie Bigar, Paulette Battenfelder, Joan Carson, Art Carey, Janet Weiss, Denise Easton, Ken Daly, Georgia Donovan, Carol Forman, Tim Durkin, Marty Faigus, Dixie Eng, Bev Galloway, Ruth Ferber, Molly Hoyle, Adrienne Gioe, Dale Burg, Donna Greenberg, Martha Gay, Marie Izzo, Judy Peterson, Nessa Forman, Joseph Gambardello, Bob Gero, Anna Loh, Antoinette Lara, Susan Kelly, Connie Solomon, Donna Brennan, Frank Farnesi, Jean Valente, Julia Fisher, Karen Kopecky, Lil Swanson, Maggie Babb, Mary Dungan, Pam Streeter, and Eo Omwake.

Introduction

"She's just not a class act," the senior executive at a major international company said. "But we're willing to invest in her as a person as well as for our company. Can't you do something? Teach her how to behave? Can't you teach her how to handle herself in and out of the office?"

That single telephone call started me on a path of private coaching. On the surface, I was supposed to teach individuals etiquette skills. But, for me, etiquette skills cannot exist in a vacuum. Etiquette gets its authority from important, fundamental principles: respect for ourselves and respect for every other human being.

Good manners come from the inside. They reflect the principles of self-respect and respect for others. They give us confidence.

Etiquette, on the other hand, comes from outside—etiquette is merely a set of practical rules that guide our behavior with others. Knowing how we're expected to behave makes us confident and self-assured. Knowing the rules and living by them allows us to focus on the business at hand more effectively.

The young woman, my first official coaching client, graduated from an Ivy League college and a first-class MBA program. Yet those esteemed institutions failed her, as they fail many people, by ignoring the human interactions that consitute business life. Those human interactions are filled with opportunities that so often descend into minefields, simply because we have stopped reflecting on how we treat each other. We have stopped reflecting on why we make choices. We have stopped reflecting, period.

"As within, so without" is more true today than ever. Although I am a cheerleader for our miraculous technology, I think it's a great loss that we no longer have any down time. It seems to me that we have traded our compassion, kindness, and consideration towards others for quantity and speed of information.

We didn't wake up one morning and decide, "Today I'm going to jettison those moments I use to collect my thoughts and center myself. Instead, I'll go out and buy a new whiz-bang gizmo so I can shop, plan a vacation, check my portfolio, handle my e-mails, order dinner, and buy theater tickets while I travel the twenty minutes from the office to home."

Our time to decompress has been eroding quietly as more technology becomes available, as the Internet expands our work pattern to "24/7."

We must realize that for every action, there is an equal and opposite reaction. If we are going to seek more and more information, then we need to allow ourselves the time to process it. We need to respond rather than react, and that takes some reflection so we can arrive at a mindset that creates win-wins.

Once we establish a mindset, then the mechanics easily support it.

Thus, good manners create good relationships and good relationships create good business. It's not the other way around.

I have received many pleas for help from people who are extraordinarily talented and productive but have a knack for alienating just about everyone—colleagues and clients alike.

That same woman, my first coaching assignment, is now a highly successful executive—both in her personal and professional lives.

Enormous challenges and hugely painful losses have punctuated my own life. Sheer survival required equal amounts of faith and a willingness to grow and explore my personal development. There were plenty of dark nights of the soul. Yet these also were gifts, because they brought me here.

I have been able to share—with my first coaching client and those that followed her—the important lessons I've learned along the way.

The examples set by my personal heroes, the principles that have come to guide me, and the points of view that express my heart and soul are what I bring to all of my relationships. Based on my clients' feedback over the years, those things meant as much if not more to them than any checklist of etiquette do's and don'ts.

And so I share them here, with you.

Part I

WHAT IS A CLASS ACT

CHAPTER 1

The Constants, from Children to CEOs

"We must become the change we wish to see in the world."
—Mahatma Gandhi

I have been a corporate trainer, consultant, and coach for more than a decade. That makes me a people-watcher of the first order, and I have met quite a few "class acts"—people who live civil, successful, and centered lives.

I have my own set of criteria, but I wanted a broader definition and asked everyone on my address list to define the qualities of a class act—an ideal business person. I was astounded by the variety, clarity, and depth of their responses. People I'd not heard from in months shot back wonderfully articulate replies. Clearly, I had struck a chord.

Here is what I learned. Here is what I have to share.

WHAT IS A CLASS ACT TO MARY MITCHELL?

When I was a guest on the ABC network show *Good Morning, America,* the host asked me to list the five skills every child should acquire to grow into a successful adult. My response:

1. Say "please," "thank you," "and excuse me."

2. Shake hands, make eye contact, and introduce themselves and others.

3. Learn how to give and receive both praise and criticism.

4. Respect everyone, and make fun of no one.

5. Use basic table manners.

6. Always be accurate.

7. Accept responsibility for your conduct.

Why? Because no matter how technologically savvy we become, no matter how time-crunched, downsized, and stressed out, the fact remains that people are people. If you cut me, I bleed. If you disrespect me, I am hurt. The best people never forget this. They are confident that helping others brings its own rewards. They are effective with others because they know how they are expected to behave in any given situation and thus are sufficiently at ease to make a real difference. That's why learning the rules of etiquette makes sense; they serve as a foundation for living a civil, centered, and successful life.

So, yes, this can be described as a book of etiquette information. And it is much more than that. Without a genuine respect for the ideas, integrity, property, and time of others, etiquette rules are hollow at best. Simply knowing the rules of etiquette will not turn someone into a role model for living well.

This is because we are talking about acting and not about thinking. The world judges us by our actions, not our thoughts. So the most successful business people are obviously people of action, who lead by example and show us all how it can be done. And while it may not be as transparent, they all try to consider other people first.

They have their priorities straight. They are responsible. What I know beyond all doubt is that when I've got my priorities straight, my life works. I'm centered. When they're askew, nothing seems to work.

It comes down to this: good manners create good relationships, and good relationships create good business. It's definitely not the other way around.

REMAINING A CLASS ACT, EVEN THROUGH CRISES

We all struggle through temporary crises that cause us to lapse. Yet, in the big picture, here's how it works in my life, in the following order.

- First, I recognize that I am part of a much bigger plan, a child of my Creator. When I feel like slugging someone and being nasty—which happens far more often than I'd like to admit—I have to stop myself and remember that the greater part of me was not born nasty.

- Second is my relationship with myself. That means staying healthy, keeping fit, telling the truth to myself and others. It means staying centered. It means not breaking my word, doing what I say I will, and being willing to admit when I'm wrong. It means being able to laugh at myself when I do goofy things. Sometimes forgiving myself for the times I slip up is not as easy as forgiving others' mistakes.

- Next comes my relationship with my spouse, followed by my relationships with family and friends. Support doesn't necessarily mean agreement. It's easy to respect and honor them when they're doing what I want them to do. The challenge—and the grace—come in when that's not so.

- Finally, there's the relationship with my work. Ah, there's the rub. I am as guilty as anybody of putting work way ahead of anything else, of anyone else. From time to time, we must . . . for a while. It's when that becomes standard operating procedure that we get ourselves into trouble. We stop being centered.

As Eleanor Roosevelt said, "To handle yourself, use your head; to handle others, use your heart." When we're centered, we can balance head and heart and create win-win relationships.

WHAT IS A CLASS ACT TO OTHERS?

I conducted a survey among people I admire and respect by asking, "When you hear a businessperson described as a 'class act,' what attributes, qualities, characteristics, and descriptions come to mind?"

Their responses were wonderful and varied:

- An impeccable communicator who knows exactly what each word, phrase, intonation, and gesture means. Listens well and expresses interest in the ideas of co-workers and subordinates, not just superiors. Articulate without being pretentious or affected. Looks you straight in the eye.

- Someone who is fair and straightforward. Accepts responsibility and does not look for someone to blame when a problem arises. Has set clear boundaries that should not be crossed, yet is flexible when compromise is necessary. Behaves consistently, without resorting to shouting or tirades.

- Experienced and astute but knows when to ask for assistance. Has the confidence to let others shine more brightly. Has a solid track record but does not boast about it.

- Sets about to achieve individual or company-related professional goals in a way that does not harm or cheat others. Cares about what's going on in colleagues' lives away from the office.

- Personable and polite and knows how to put people at ease. Inherently kind and generous, with a presence that is strong but not overpowering.

- Has a clever sense of humor—does not take himself/herself too seriously. Never puts down anyone or tries for a laugh at the expense of others.

- Socially savvy and courteous, with good table manners. Dresses with style, grace, and always appropriately. Says thanks in public, writes notes, and makes calls of gratitude.

- Honest and a model of integrity. Can be trusted at all times and has high standards. Is thoughtful, compassionate, considerate, and sincere. Returns calls and e-mails on the same day.

- Offers to do and does favors for others, especially for their children and other family members. Looks for opportunities to return favors.

- Is direct; delivers good news and bad in a no-nonsense yet sensitive way. Speaks to be understood by the audience at hand—doesn't use jargon outside his/her industry/organization; looks for ways to put others at ease.

READ ON AND YOU WILL LEARN WHAT IT TAKES TO BE A CLASS ACT.

CHAPTER 2

A Class Act Has Self-Confidence

"There is overwhelming evidence that the higher the level of self-esteem, the more likely one will be to treat others with respect, kindness, and generosity"

—Nathaniel Branden

You can't make chicken salad from chicken feathers. And one does not become a Class Act simply by wishing it were so. There are some fundamentals that need to be in place as a foundation on which to construct the business person you wish to become. Let's start with:

CONFIDENCE

The dictionary defines confidence as trust or faith, being sure. I believe it means feeling good about yourself, especially in regard to accomplishing something. Which something? It can be a new job, a new assignment, a performance review, networking, or a meeting with co-workers.

Here are some things we can do right now to build up our confidence quotients.

MOVEMENT

No, not to a new job or neighborhood. Movement means exercise, literally. Move your body. Take the stairs instead of the elevator. Park farther away from the store you're about to visit, and walk the distance.

Walk. Run. Ride a bike. Lift weights, even if it means doing your reps with a five-pound bag of flour in each hand. Work up a sweat. You'll feel better.

Exercise clears the brain and the lungs, making room for new, better, possibly bolder thoughts. It gives us more energy. And let's face it; energy is attractive. Energetic people magnetize others. When we feel better, we become more confident.

Nothing enhances your overall appearance like being fit. A regular regimen of exercise improves not only your posture but your personality. Fit people look more focused and more confident. Becoming physically fit and participating in sports helps further careers.

Exercise also increases strength and endurance and helps mightily to defuse anger and frustration and get the creative juices flowing.

ATTIRE AND GROOMING

There is no such thing as neutral clothing. Everything you put on represents a decision you have made and is a reflection of your taste, your sense, and your style. Think about the type of clothes you wear.

If your attire is inappropriate, colleagues are prone to question whether you know the rules of the game and whether or not you are likely to be a significant player. Your superiors are apt to conclude that the quality of your work will match the quality of your appearance.

When you're considering how to dress for a particular work situation, ask yourself these questions: Who am I? What role am I playing? How do I want to be perceived? What will be the setting? Who are the people I want to impress favorably?

We're not talking about fashion statements, we're talking about what image works effectively in a given environment.

In order to always project a great appearance, develop key relationships with a:

1. Tailor. Excellent tailors are increasingly difficult to find, but well worth hunting down. Good fit can make an inexpensive garment look like a million, and a poor fit can make even an Armani look sloppy.
2. Dry cleaner. Dry cleaning is not good for fabrics, so protect your clothing investment and find a reliable dry cleaner.
3. Shoemaker. Everybody notices shoes, mostly because we often get nervous and end up looking at the floor. Keep shoes well shined and in good repair.
4. Dentist. Find a dentist you like and go regularly. A clean, bright smile goes a long way in completing the perfect appearance.

BREATHING

Breathing is the essence of life, and a key to fueling a confident Class Act. Find sanctuary inside yourself. There is honor in standing still. We are so time-crunched, information-bludgeoned, downsized, and multi-tasked that it's spiritually suffocating. Who we really are comes from the inside out. Without a way to "go inside" and focus, we add to our environment's chaos rather than its harmony. Learn "belly breathing": lie down on the floor, be quiet, and place your hands on your stomach.

Breathe from your belly, letting it rise and fall like a bellows. Babies breathe this way, and we know how self-confident they are. Men breathe this way, too. I've learned to belly breathe on elevators, in restroom stalls, and in the middle of crowded rooms when I need to calm down and focus. No need to chant "om."

SELF-DISCIPLINE

Keep your agreements. Be on time. Be mindful and in the present. These are gifts to yourself as well as others. Whatever we think and feel right now creates what happens in the future. When we stick to the "now" and don't chase rabbits, we are involved and aware of opportunities and others will sense that we're fully with them. This has a tremendous impact on the quality of all personal and professional relationships.

GIVING AND RECEIVING

Give what you want to get in return. If you want cooperation and respect, give respect and cooperate. If you want to succeed, help others succeed. If you want more joy, be more joyful. When we circulate our positive energy, we create more and more to enjoy. Be open to giving to yourself. Honor your own worthiness to receive; if you don't, no one else will.

Perhaps you are thinking, "Yeah, so tell me something I don't know already."

I learned from one of my teachers that successful people do what they know, so practice what you know and you will come across as the successful person you are . . . and build the foundation for your life as a Class Act!

CHAPTER 3

A Class Act Exemplifies the Virtues of Accountability and Forgiveness

"How far you go in life depends on you being tender with the young, compassionate with the aged, sympathetic with the striving, and tolerant of the weak and the strong. Because someday in life you will have been all of these."

—George Washington Carver

To be a Class Act, you need to "walk your talk." What do I mean by that? It comes down to the simple idea that we are what we do and not who we say we are. Being able to express a philosophy is far easier than to act on those principles. A friend of mine says that we can't think our way into right living, but we can act our way into right thinking.

Colleagues trust each other less and less these days, and one reason is that people often speak one way and act another. The pressure to produce, coupled with a fear of being laid off at the next economic downturn, or of a big company disintegrating in a matter of months like Enron, have contributed to the me-first atmosphere of "I'll help you out so long as it doesn't hurt me."

What do experienced workers gain by voluntarily guiding recent college graduates or other newcomers through the company maze to better-paying jobs? The risk, that they might just be training their own replacement, is seen as too high. That engenders a stale, if not sterile, workplace where people are just putting in time and minding their own business.

According to *Trust and Betrayal in the Workplace,* by Dennis S. Reina and Michelle L. Reina, (Berrett-Koehler, December 1999), "After years of downsizing, restructuring, mergers and growth, trust among people at every level is at an all-time low."

How sad. Is there anything worse to say about people than "I don't trust them?" Not to me. In the bigger scheme of things, this lack of workplace trust comes at a heavy price. If we don't trust our colleagues, we won't allow ourselves to be creative or to take risks. Productivity plummets. So does efficiency.

The Reinas ask the following questions to help determine just how trustworthy you and your colleagues are. Use your answers to determine if you are walking your talk.

- Do you keep your agreements? Do you do what you say you will, or do you constantly renegotiate or renege on your promises?

- Do you spell out precisely what you will do yourself and what you expect of others?

- Are you consistent in your behavior? Do your actions match your words, or do you send out mixed messages with a double standard?

- Do you share information that others need to do their jobs, or do you hoard it for yourself to enhance feelings of power?

- Do you openly admit mistakes, or do you try to cover them up or place blame on others?

- Do you encourage constructive feedback with the intention of helping others?

- Do you gossip behind co-workers' backs?

- Do you acknowledge the skills and abilities of others? Do you trust them to do their jobs or do you try to micromanage them?

- Do you openly acknowledge the work of others when you use it or incorporate it into yours?

MEET A BULLYING BOSS

Joe C. was a bully, a tyrant, a nasty little man who delighted in gossip and making subordinates squirm. He raged. His sarcasm reached uncharted depths and no human frailty or shortcoming escaped his mean comments, always made in front of others. He ruled by intimidation. He never made a mistake (and he'd be the first to tell you so in one way or another). He trusted no one. He had wild mood swings and played favorites.

Joe C. was my boss early in my career. Healing from a divorce was easy compared to healing the wounds he inflicted on my psyche, self-esteem, and self-confidence. Without exaggeration, the man haunted my dreams—he knew every single button to push on this timid young woman who had been brought up in convent schools. Fully a year after I left his employ (he fired me, of course), I was bemoaning the experience to a friend who said, "Do you realize you're even sleeping with this jerk? You let him get to you so much that you dream about him. Why don't you just let it go and forgive the poor pig?"

Talk about wanting to shoot the messenger! Forgive Joe C.? Hell would freeze over first. She actually wanted me to turn the other cheek and make it okay that he abused me? She must be crazy, I thought.

I thought wrong. And I felt wrong. I had no concept of the power of forgiveness. Nor did I have any idea how it could transform my life. I was so stuck in my self-righteousness that I couldn't (wouldn't?) let bygones be bygones. Looking back all those years ago, I see that Joe C. was in fact a blessing. Without his mistreatment, I might never have gotten onto a career that's been all I've wanted mine to be. I have no idea what's become of him. It would be nice to think that he has changed, too. But I can't change anybody else. I only can change me.

FORGIVENESS DEFINED

Forgiveness doesn't mean letting someone off the hook. It is the willing-ness and ability to understand what motivates someone's actions. It is let-ting go of the hurt and concentrating on moving forward. It means giving up being angry and the desire to strike back. Forgiveness is a gift to oneself.

Forgiveness is a gift that pays off not only in terms of our psyche; it relieves stress and aids in sleeping as well as in creativity. Forgive and you'll be hap-pier and have more energy in the long run.

THE MECHANICS OF FORGIVENESS

According to Stanford University psychologist Carl Thoresen, even the most grudge-bearing people can learn to forgive. Here are his suggestions:

1. Accept that no adult can control another's behavior. Shift from one's own rigid rules about how people should behave to "preferences." We may expect the people closest to us to be perfect, yet we must allow them to be imperfect. We need to ask ourselves honestly if a relationship is one we'd be better off without.
2. Look at the hurtful incident in perspective. Situations are neutral. It's the emotion and feeling we bring to them that gives them significance. Be willing to see something from the other person's point of view.
3. Move away from blame to acceptance, and then move forward.

What You Can Do

It's important to express yourself and say when you are angry, disappointed, or sad. Otherwise, these feelings build up and turn into resentment. That might sound like, "When you do _____, I feel _____." There are creative ways to express anger, such as talking it out with a friend or family member, taking long walks, or writing a "stream-of-consciousness" letter (that you never mail).

RESPONSIBILITY

An eleven-year-old once wrote to my newspaper column to ask what I thought responsibility meant for young people like him. I was very grateful for the question, as it made me define my foundation for a civil, serene, and successful life.

I really believe the duties of an eleven-year-old are basically the same as for an adult. Life gets more complicated as we get older, but being responsible is the underlying key, whether you're a CEO or a boy scout.

Being Responsible Means

- that when I feel mean or nasty, I have to stop myself and remember that the greater part of me was not born mean and nasty.

- being true to myself—staying healthy, keeping fit, and telling the truth to myself and to others.

- keeping my word, doing what I say I will, and being willing to admit when I'm wrong.

- being willing to laugh at myself when I do goofy things.

- that I have to try to be the best person I can be and not be too hard on myself when I slip up.

- respecting and honoring members of my family, even when it is hard and I don't agree with them.

- supporting and sticking by my friends and being willing to share my ups and downs with them.

- accepting whatever responsibilities are there for me—such as my marriage and my job—and treating all people in my life with as much kindness, dignity, and respect as I would like them to show me.

The Ten Commandments of Responsible Business Behavior

1. Thou shalt have a positive attitude.
2. Thou shalt be on time.
3. Thou shalt take clear and correct messages.

4. Thou shalt praise in public and criticize in private.
5. Thou shalt not invade anyone's space with thy cell phone, nor multi-task while on the phone.
6. Thou shalt take the time to remember people's names.
7. Thou shalt not use foul language, slang, or bad grammar.
8. Thou shalt dress appropriately.
9. Thou shalt use good table manners.
10. Thou shalt be accountable and take responsibility for both accomplishments and mistakes.

CHAPTER 4

A Class Act Exemplifies
the Virtue of Trustworthiness

"The moment we break faith with one another, the sea engulfs us and the light goes out."

—James Baldwin

SECRETS, SACRED SECRETS

It feels wonderful to tell a secret. It feels wonderful to hear one. In the telling, we feel empowered. In the receiving, we feel special and singular. The secret binds us. It makes fellows of us.

Noted Swiss physician Paul Tournier maintains that secrets are vital to our lives, enabling the maturation process. He wrote, "Every human being needs secrecy in order to become himself and no longer only a member of the tribe . . . What grants secrecy its capital value is that individuality is at stake and every violation of secrecy is a violation of that individuality . . . Respect for the individual is an absolute requirement. Either we have the sense of it and keep it scrupulously, or else we have started down the dangerous road of tyranny."

Respecting and Keeping Boundaries

Growing up, I was amazed that my mother steadfastly refused to look at another person's private papers and messages, even when they were in plain view. I remember when I was helping her to clean my sister's room and we found her diary, open on the desk. This, I thought, was a gold mine, surely a gift from on high to provide me with blackmailing material for the foreseeable future. I took the bait instantly, only to be roundly scolded and punished for my action.

What this lesson taught me was that reading anything that doesn't belong to you is the worst form of stealing, and it means that one who does this cannot be trusted. If you cannot be trusted, it doesn't much matter what else you can do. Violating a confidence is a contemptuous thing to do. It crushes the trust in a relationship. Once trust is gone, nothing worthwhile remains.

GOSSIP: SECOND-HAND POISON

Ever notice how we put forth piety as we snipe? We say things like, "I really don't know whether this is true or not, but . . . ." In short, we allege to resist the urge to gossip all the while we insist on doing so.

"I want to deal with people I trust, people who don't say bad or malicious things about anybody. I figure they won't say anything bad about me, either." Marty Faigus, my friend and attorney who's helped me navigate the shoals of intellectual property challenges, made this comment almost off-handedly. How true it is—and how it made me think.

My friends often are my role models. Jane Dalton, another attorney friend, comes to mind when I think about trustworthiness and integrity and some-one who doesn't gossip. In the 15 years we've been friends, I have always been struck by how her integrity makes her a true leader. As the first woman partner in a major Philadelphia law firm with offices worldwide, and a direc-tor of the Philadelphia Bar Association, she can be as tough and resolute as they come. Yet I have yet to hear a bad word about her, she doesn't need to raise her voice to make points, and she is never mean-spirited.

WHAT MAKES STAND-UP PEOPLE STAND OUT

Stand-up people don't initiate gossip and they don't encourage anyone else to gossip. They don't repeat gossip they happen to hear to anyone else. They defend victims of gossip whenever they can.

Negative gossip surrounds us. Rumors abound. Remember that game we played when we were kids. We called it "Whisper Down The Lane." Some called it "Telephone." People seem to thrive on repeating stories that can hurt and harm. With each telling, the truth becomes embellished and editorialized. Pretty soon the innocent tale of John leaving his office upset and in a hurry because his child was taken to the emergency room becomes JOHN STALKS OUT, FURIOUS THAT BOSS ARGUED THE POINT, SLAMMING THE DOOR BEHIND HIM, NOT CARING ABOUT THE CONSEQUENCES. Suddenly it's a headline and people begin agreeing that it "sounds just like him, a hot-head. It's probably true and who knows who suffered in the outcome?" Pretty soon poor John sounds like an irresponsible employee with a temper = a disaster waiting to happen = undesirable.

GOSSIP

Let's think about the kinds of gossip we encounter. Three levels come to mind: first, idle chatter of little or no consequence to anyone; second, idle chatter that is hurtful to others, although not intentionally used as such by the speaker; and third, mean-spirited, directed commentary.

Time is precious. Gossip wastes time and hurts innocent people. I can list dozens of more productive things to do with my work time. Besides, gossip can jettison someone's career ascent or reputation or both. Some might argue that gossiping based on false facts or hearsay is criminal, because it harms innocent people. Personally, I just believe that we attract whatever we give our attention to. So if we spend a lot of time jabbering about John's "senseless" departure from the office, and speculate about the negative consequences (e.g., "If I were his supervisor, he'd be toast."), eventually it happens in one way or another.

Bird-brained, mindless gossip is just silly and makes the taleteller look far worse than the target. Does it really matter how many cosmetic surgeries someone has had, for example? OK, so this might be tasty "dish," yet does it really contribute anything to anybody? Besides, don't we sound a lot more informed, interested, and interesting if we dish about new movies or sports events?

When we're speculating about serious issues, we'd better zip our skeptical lips. Let's say you don't quite believe that someone's credentials are all someone claims. (A bit envious, are we?) Voicing your suspicions can cause trouble. And you'll look like a fool if and when you're proved wrong.

STOP THE GOSSIP

Take the high road and do not engage in the game. Nothing infuriates and frustrates a gossip more than not taking the bait. Here's how:

1. Change the topic of conversation. Precious time is on your side. That might sound like, "Listen, pals, life is too short to get entangled in this stuff. Besides, I really need to know your thoughts on . . . solution to . . . opinion of. . . . We've got goals to meet."
2. Drift away. You don't need to say a word. Just remove yourself from the scene, i.e., the group of chatterers. Your silence and absence will be eloquent.
3. Rise to the defense. Say things like, "Listen, this just doesn't sound like John." Or, "That really isn't the way I heard it." Then, "It's really not fair to belabor this when John can't be here to defend himself." Note: Avoid saying, "You are unfair, etc." The moment we begin a sentence with

"you," communication stops while the other person builds a defense.

4. Speak the truth to the right person. When you learn that a rumor is untrue, take the person who is spreading it around aside and straighten the score. That might sound like, "I thought you'd be interested to know that, as a matter of fact, John really was editor of the *Harvard Law Review*. So it's a good idea to stop entertaining conversations that he wasn't." Period. No lecturing; just the facts, spoken in as unemotional and flat a tone as though you were saying, "It's raining outside."

5. Deflect, don't report. No good can come of repeating petty rumors to those being rumored about. It just hurts, and there's the clear and present danger that the messenger will be shot. When you hear a serious untruth being spread about someone, immediately and passionately rise to the defense. That might sound like, "I don't believe that information for a single moment. If it does happen to be true, there must have been a very good reason for it that we do not know. What I do know is that I am not willing to stand here and be a party to a story that maligns a good person. Get somebody else to listen."

I advise you to heed two aphorisms that George Washington copied in his book, *Rules of Civility and Decent Behaviour in Company and Conversation*:

Let your conversation be without malice or envy, for it is a sign of a tractable and commendable nature; and, in all cases of passion, admit reason to govern.

A CLASS ACT IS ALWAYS CIVIL AND TRUSTWORTHY.

CHAPTER 5

Why a Corporation Must Also Be a Class Act

"Noblesse Oblige" (Rank Compels Obligation)
—Duc de Levis, 1764-1830

Currently, camouflaging losses under the heading of expenses or outside real-estate ventures may send some executives behind bars, yet putting all of the legal proceedings aside, we are learning about some very arrogant, greedy, and downright rude people.

Sadly, these rude individuals—the corporate executives, directors, lawyers, accountants—need to be reminded of noblesse oblige, or that rank, their rank specifically, compels obligation. Remembering this would help bring into focus their duties and responsibilities.

After all, corporations are entities made up of individuals, people like you and me.

Boards of directors govern corporations. Those directors are individuals, real people like you and me. It is their job to govern the corporation on behalf of the corporation's stockholders who have elected them. The stockholders are individuals, people like you and me—no more and no less.

In 2002, "corporate governance" seems to be the buzzword du jour. The media can't get enough of it. With the messes produced at Enron, World-Com, Global Crossing, and far too many other firms, the legalistic phrase appears daily in the press. It all sounds very high-minded, intellectual, and inscrutable. While this upheaval will pass, another will eventually follow as the darkness comes after light.

Just what is corporate governance? I suggest that it is simply—yet not easily—corporate manners.

Good manners are about treating others the way we want to be treated. Is it not rude to think only of oneself? Yet is that not what happens when corporate officers report inaccurate financial results? An individual with good manners is responsible for his conduct and the consequences of his behavior. Individuals with good manners define themselves by their actions; their words merely support their behavior.

We trust individuals who treat others the way they wish to be treated.

Class Acts is intended for individuals, but to place the matter in a broader context, let's also consider the conduct of many individuals' employer: The Corporation.

The relevance and notice given the concepts and standards of proper corporate governance have been elevated in recent years to the point that, at the beginning of the 21st century, they are at the heart of a critical public issue.

WHAT IS CORPORATE GOVERNANCE?

I suggest it is no more nor less than corporate manners—and now we find that this "body guard of manners" is of paramount importance to the constituencies the corporation serves. In fact corporate executives and directors need only be reminded of noblesse oblige—rank compels obligation—to place their duties and responsibilities in focus.

While the entire *Class Acts* text applies to individual persons in the corporate structure—management, directors, employees—I suggest that the overriding structure of rules by which a civil society exists applies separately as well as equally to the fictitious person: the corporation.

THE CONSTITUENCIES (READ "PEOPLE")

These examples illustrate why corporate Class Act-ness is so important to so many. The damage from bad governance is direct and swift.

1. Stockholders, who through their elected directors chose the executives leading the companies whose shares they own, stand to lose on their equity investments.
2. Employees whose jobs, work environment, and life security are entrusted to the executives are paying for the corporate executives' lack of good manners with their jobs, their pensions, or sometimes even their lives.
3. Directors who are financially and personally responsible for the business conduct of the executives also lose when the bad judgments and their consequences surface.
4. Suppliers whose businesses, financial stability, and operations are damaged by the actions of the executives who rudely ignore the obligations imposed by the code of noblesse oblige.
5. Retirees who depend on the good governance of the corporation may lose pension benefits, their personal retirement investments in their company's stock, and retiree medical plans when rudeness rules.
6. Communities in which a corporation has offices, plants, or other facilities stand to lose a significant corporate citizen, employer, and taxpayer when the company's leaders fail to understand or choose to ignore noblesse oblige.
7. Other investors, such as bondholders, partners in joint ventures, and franchise holders, all depend on good governance to protect and enhance their investments—and rudeness will negatively impact each of them.
8. Consultants are subject to financial loss and professional destruction when their corporate clients are governed without regard to good manners and when the resulting misinformation, fraud, and collapse are laid at their doors.
9. Banks and other financial institutions may sink under the weight of bad loans, bad accounting, corrupt business practices, and fraud upon their institutions brought on by bad client governance—again a denial of the obligations of rank to practice integrity.
10. Management itself ultimately pays because of stock options that can become worthless, lost employment for themselves, criminal prosecution or civil lawsuits, private civil actions for damages—again because of rude behavior.
11. Customers, such as the U.S. government, are dependent upon the uninterrupted services under contract, and serious consequences may result

from the bankruptcy status caused by accounting fraud—again simple rudeness and arrogance of the executives.

In short, responsible corporate governance is best ensured by good manners. The consequences of the lack of ethical standards and infectious greed are reported daily in the financial press. Now we have plunging stock prices, bankruptcies, government investigations, congressional hearings, and new legislative proposals. All this may eventually persuade a misinformed corporate culture that the principle of noblesse oblige practiced with good manners will eventually restore financial prosperity and maintain it when it does reappear.

What about considering this solution? Each individual is responsible for his conduct and its consequences. We are what we do. Our actions speak louder than our words. Our acts, not our words, define and reveal us.

Or, simpler still, consider this: Do unto others as you would have them do unto you.

Congressional actions, criminal punishments, civil fines, or regulatory fiats never truly will change the system. The corporate governance culture must be reborn with respect for truth, accountability, integrity, accuracy, and honor. As long as we chase the paradigm of greed, avarice, and fraud, rude corporate governance will flourish.

As investors, we demand accountability more than ever. We have stopped trusting. Until we can comfortably believe corporate numbers, results, statements, earnings, etc., the market will continue to stagnate. We will put our money elsewhere than corporate America.

When corporate management reports inaccurate financial results, engages in self-dealing, is less than candid to its Board, outside constituents etc., it amounts to corporate rudeness. How very sad.

CONCLUSION

You can now understand that the following chapters, which illustrate the many characteristics of a Class Act, apply to corporate conduct as well.

Consider the New Paradigm

Bad corporate governance is, in fact, corporate rudeness. And good corporate governance is, in fact, good manners.

A CLASS ACT CORPORATION IS TRUSTED BY ALL THE PEOPLE WHOSE LIVES IT TOUCHES.

CHAPTER 6

A Class Act Is Never Rude

"Life is not so short but that there is always time enough for courtesy."
—Ralph Waldo Emerson

In all facets of our working and personal lives, there is a price paid for rudeness. And the cost is seen in the bottom line of companies and the erosion of even the best of relationships.

The April 2002 report of the Public Agenda Foundation—"Aggravating Circumstances—A Status Report on Rudeness in America"—brings this issue of rudeness into current focus. The results of their intensive survey (by questionnaire) of more than 2,000 members of the public, focus groups in seven U.S. cities, and a series of one-on-one in-depth interviews before and after the study was completed resulted in these easy to follow rules for overcoming rudeness.

One: Just a Little Common Courtesy

Americans say that disrespect, lack of consideration, and rudeness are serious, pervasive problems that affect them on a personal, gut level. People acknowledge that Americans' behavior has improved in some areas, such as the treatment of racial and ethnic minorities and the disabled. Americans say they are witnessing a deterioration of courtesy and respectfulness that has become a daily assault on their sensibilities and the quality of their lives.

Two: Bad for Business

Americans say that the way they are treated by business and customer-service employees is frequently exasperating and sometimes even insulting. Too many workers, they complain, are careless, apathetic, and unhelpful. Almost half of those surveyed say that they have walked out of a business specifically because of bad service, and the number is even higher among affluent Americans.

Three: Driven to Distraction

If Americans are exasperated by the way that businesses and government agencies treat them, they are equally disenchanted with the behavior of many of their fellow citizens. Majorities of Americans complain about inconsiderate, even dangerous drivers; rude cell-phone users; and a virtually ubiquitous onslaught of profanity and coarse language.

Four: As the Twig Is Bent

Americans are particularly concerned about the discourteous and disrespectful conduct of children, and they hold parents primarily responsible for this phenomenon. People say that too many parents don't invest the energy needed to teach their children good behavior, and that too often they fail to set a good example themselves. But even when parents try hard, Americans say, social forces—especially in popular culture and the entertainment media—routinely undercut their efforts.

Five: Why Are So Many People Rude?

Americans point to a confluence of different factors to explain the deterioration of courtesy and respectfulness in today's world. In part, they say, too much crowding, too much anonymity, and the pressures of fast-paced lives invite rude behavior, and then rudeness begets more rudeness. Other explanations point to the times we live in and the values we live by—a declining sense of community, offensive and amoral entertainment media, and an over-all rise in selfishness and callousness.

Six: The Day Things Changed

The shock and loss of September 11, 2001, changed the behavior of Americans for the better, most people believe, but they also suspect that the change will be relatively short-lived. Many expect that we'll soon return to business as usual, if we haven't already done so.

As a result, the importance of "never be rude" is dramatically heightened.

HOW RUDENESS REALLY AFFECTS BUSINESS

My company, The Mitchell Organization, surveyed 200 major U.S. businesses to get a handle on the dynamics between consumer and supplier that create, advance, hinder, or kill a business relationship.

We learned that product, price, and quality did not make the top ten. Instead, we found that both individuals and companies make their decisions based on how well they are treated and the relationships they form with the people in that company. What this means for you is that you should try to combine your business sense and advice with a dose of kindness, because good manners create good relationships—and good relationships create good business.

THE TEN MOST COMMON BUSINESS MISTAKES TO AVOID

1. Negative Attitudes

This top complaint manifests itself in many different ways including rudeness, impoliteness, "taking it out on someone," bitchiness, surliness, bad temperament, unprovoked anger, and unpleasantness. Words and actions have an effect on others. No one's life is exempt from stress or frustration; they are guaranteed, just like death and taxes.

With a little self-control and consideration, though, the same "nasty" person might find support and sympathy for whatever is upsetting them. By being rude, they are just making things worse for themselves and the people around them. At best, they are further distancing themselves from a solution; at worst, they are jeopardizing their careers. And all of this reflects right back up to the top of the organization.

2. Sloppy Telephone Communication and Message Taking

Bosses gripe that they don't get clear, correct, or complete messages. Support staff complain that callers talk down to them and don't want to answer their questions. And callers are unhappy with support staff who are brusque, won't take detailed messages, and are uninformed as to when their boss might be able to call them back.

Just as truck drivers are trained and tested before they are allowed on the road, we need to teach everyone how to use the telephone properly. Communication is just as important as transportation in business, and the phone is the main vehicle of business communication.

Think, too, of the time that is wasted on trying to return calls with faulty information from poorly taken messages. Calling wrong numbers, apologizing to people whose names you are not sure of, calling someone daily only to discover that they were on vacation—if phone skills improved, business could save millions of hours and dollars.

3. Making People Wait

Being put on "hold" indefinitely on the telephone, without being asked if you would like to "hold" or told how long it will take your desired party to speak to you, or being kept waiting, without an explanation, for a scheduled appointment, creates resentment and sets a hostile tone for the ensuing conversation.

Making people wait is a manipulative power play, even though in some cases it may not be intentional.

The simple solution is to take thirty seconds—it literally takes no longer than that—to give the waiting party an update and ask if they would like to continue to wait or reschedule / call back. As with most problems, an ounce of prevention is worth a pound of cure. In this case, an ounce of courtesy avoids a pound of bad feeling.

4. Criticizing People in Front of Others

Giving and taking constructive criticism, even in private, is a difficult skill for many people to master, because it requires maturity and openness on the part of both parties.

If in a business meeting or confrontation the intent is to improve a situation or encourage someone to grow, public criticism doesn't work. This behavior serves no purpose except to breed ill will and cutthroat competitiveness. These "Machiavellian manners" are losing favor in this new century, which is becoming concerned with personal civility and corporate ethics.

5. Disregarding Invitation Requests

Business people show disrespect if they do not RSVP promptly, if at all, or assume that they can bring uninvited guests. So be sure to always respond promptly, usually in the same form as the invitation was given: i.e., a written reply to a written invitation, a telephone call in reply to same, and so forth. You can always ask if you might bring along X, explaining why you are making the request, and of course abiding by the invitation giver's decision with graciousness.

6. Errors with Peoples' Names and Titles

Pronouncing and spelling a person's name correctly is important. If you can't get something as simple as a name and title right, a superior or client may wonder what else you will be careless about.

In business, you must also be aware of the inappropriate use of first names, assuming familiarity when it is not justified or desired.

7. Vulgar Language

In today's workplace, you can witness the deterioration of verbal skills, evidenced especially in the use of four-letter words and the common acceptance of foul language, poor grammar, and slang. Using proper grammar and leaving bad language out of all business conversation projects an image of professionalism and intelligence.

8. Inappropriate Clothing

Every company and industry has a dress code, even if it isn't set down in writing. When dressing for work, your individual freedom of expression must be tempered by good judgment about your appearance.

For men, remember to polish shoes, press shirts, wear suits that fit well, and remove lint from clothing.

For women, don't overdo the perfume or make-up, or wear overly revealing clothing, running shoes, or high heels with toe cleavage in the office.

Neat, clean, appropriate business dress is an important key to success.

9. Forgoing Introductions

Support staff feel insignificant when you forget to introduce them to your colleagues. Lack of an introduction, whether a peer or superior forgets it, makes people feel uncomfortable.

Taking the time to make introductions is a seemingly small action that makes a big difference in the long run to everyone's ease and attitude. Even if you have forgotten the name of any of the parties involved, that's no excuse. Simply request the name and proceed. People don't mind so much if you forget their name; they do mind it if you don't acknowledge their existence through a simple introduction.

10. Giving Someone the Run-Around

Complaints such as not being able to get an answer, being referred to ten different people, getting conflicting answers to the same question, people not listening to questions or complaints, or no one wanting to handle a special request—it's called the run-around.

Although the run-around may be unintentional, because the employee is just not informed, it helps to tell people up front if that is the case. A Class Act needs to avoid every one of the most common business behavior mistakes.

A CLASS ACT GIVES CAREFUL ATTENTION TO BOTH ACTUAL AND PERCEIVED BEHAVIOR, FORCEFULLY ESCHEWS RUDENESS IN BOTH, AND SHINES AS AN EXAMPLE OF COURTESY AND CONSIDERATION AT ALL TIMES.

Part II

LEARN A NECESSARY SKILL

CHAPTER 7

A Class Act Requires Peace

"All men's miseries derive from not being able to sit quietly in a room alone."

—Blaise Pascal

"For fast-acting relief, try 'slow down.'"

—Lily Tomlin

Peace means being able to control stress. Stress is a powerful, potent force—whether positive or negative.

We shoulder unreasonable deadlines, put in twelve-hour days and routinely skip lunch. We can't sleep. Our necks hurt, our eyes hurt, our hands hurt. As glorious as technology is, our cell phones, computers, and pagers are high-tech leashes that make it impossible to escape our jobs.

We need to breathe, to count to ten, to gain perspective, to realize that nothing really matters if we don't have our health and people in our lives who care about us. Sure, making money is great. Being the best at what we do and winning acclaim for our achievements are noble goals—but at what cost? We are suffering from information overload. We feel out of control. We are on tilt—like the pinball machine that has been pushed a little too hard, shaken over the edge. We must find a way to get off tilt, to reset ourselves in a positive position.

TUNING OUT TO TUNE IN—UNPLUGGING

If you want to be able to fire off compelling messages from your laptop, to sound assured and on top of things over your cell phone, to give a stirring speech that brings the audience to its feet, you first need to compose yourself to figure out what to say and how to say it. To do that, you need to cut out the chatter and clatter from your mind. It's essential to be centered.

MEDITATION

Meditating is like flossing. We all know it's good for us. We just don't have time for it—or at least that's what we tell ourselves. And what, if anything, does it have to do with interpersonal skills and manners, much less business success? I'll tell you.

The goal is to live in the moment, which is the only reality we know. To be able to do that—to be here, now—we need to clear our heads of the noise and confusion and clutter that sends us back ruminating over our past or into the fantasy that is the future.

Athletes call it visualization, which is simply a positive mental rehearsal of what they are about to do. Others employ the term self-hypnosis, or self talk, for the meditative state that clears their minds and brings to bear the best of what they have to offer the world. Whatever you wish to call it, meditation has as much to do with etiquette as Tiger Woods has to do with golf.

In fact, Woods, who speaks of playing one shot at a time and trying to stay in the moment, as well as Olympic medallists and other world-class athletes, have done us an enormous service by bringing meditation concepts and practices into the mainstream.

Hypnosis can be called "meditation with an attitude" and often better suits the Western mindset of immediate gratification—"I want it now, not in the next lifetime."

THE RELAXATION RESPONSE

Dr. Herbert Benson, author of the classic book *The Relaxation Response,* has proved conclusively that meditation not only lowers blood pressure; also improves cholesterol levels. Recent studies have also found that meditation relieves chronic pain and insomnia. In his book, Dr. Benson points out the two steps necessary to achieve the altered state of mind that meditation produces:

First, repetition of a word, sound, phrase, prayer, or muscular activity.

That can be as simple as breathing. To take deep, relaxing breaths, inhale from the belly, not the chest. Put one hand on your abdomen, the other on your chest. Then breathe deeply through your nose. Two inhalations for each long exhalation work best for me, done silently.

Your abdomen will expand like a balloon or a bellows. As you exhale through your mouth, let your abdomen deflate. You don't have to exaggerate either the inhalations or the exhalations; your body knows what to do. Imagine that the air you breathe in carries a sense of peace, while the air going out carries away tension and anxiety.

Second, Dr. Benson tells us that the Relaxation Response requires disregarding everyday thoughts that inevitably come to mind and returning to your repetition. This doesn't mean that you keep your mind blank. In fact, the only way your mind could be totally blank would be if you were unconscious. It just means to let your thoughts come and go and not attach to them. The goal here is to connect with your sacred gift, if you will, and not yet with the faithful servant.

DEFINITION OF TERMS

I asked my friend Barry Eisen, a Los Angeles-based consultant who works with large corporations, athletes, and government agencies, to make the distinction among hypnosis, meditation, and visualization, and this is what he said:

Visualization = mental imagery of goals, pleasing experiences and desensitizing pictures to stimulate, relax, and help you cope with life, create positive choices and to deal with negative happenings.

Hypnosis (including self-hypnosis) = a state of increased suggestibility created by relaxation (it slows down the thought process so that positive statements, images, and feelings are internalized more efficiently). This speeding up of the process of change allows for habits and attitudes to shift with greater ease. Along the way, the user of the process usually experiences greater energy (a side benefit of relaxing efficiently).

Meditation = a relaxed focus, not necessarily spiritually induced. Whether brought on by deep breathing or mantras or chants, the relaxation is usually peaceful and passive. As in hypnosis, one experiences very powerful regeneration, with endorphins zipping all over the place. It is truly uplifting.

A SIMPLE STRESS TEST

The consulting company Stress Directions has developed a test that includes a section on stress susceptibility. Test-takers respond to the following sample statements on a 1-to-5 scale, with 1 meaning "almost always," and 5 meaning "never." The higher the score, the higher the susceptibility.

- I eat at least one balanced, hot meal a day and get at least seven hours of sleep a night.

- I am in good health.

- I exercise at least twice a week.

- I regularly give and receive affection.

- I have at least one relative within fifty miles on whom I can rely.

- I organize my time effectively.

- I get strength from my spiritual beliefs.

- I do something fun at least once a week.

- I speak openly about my feelings.

- I take quiet time for myself.

- I have an optimistic outlook on life.

How did you do? Do you need to read on?

PERSONAL PREFERENCES IN PRACTICE

The lotus position is lost on me. And while repetitive chanting actually is helpful in achieving a meditative state, it isn't practical in the business arena. I found this out the hard way when I tried "oooming" in a public restroom before a speech I was about to give. It worked great in my apartment, but . . .

We have to find ways to get off tilt and back on center that work for us.

Think about what characterizes truly successful people. Are the words focus and concentration on your list? They should be.

How different is visualizing a 275-yard drive across a lake to the middle of the fairway from seeing yourself entering a roomful of strangers and leaving it with key business contacts and important leads? Or from heading home from a party where your confidence and self-assuredness won you new friends and admirers? Or from giving a compelling presentation that sparked colleagues from your own firm to offer congratulations? They all require the same skill sets. It's all in the mind.

Meditation is merely the practice of being quiet, turning your attention inward and focusing your mind. Once we connect with our intuitive mind, our "sacred gift," we then are able to put our "faithful servants" to work making better choices that result in more effective behavior.

More than a decade ago, I took a Silva Method mind development course with a friend who had breast cancer and was reaching out for alternative ways to deal with her condition. I expected something weird, some kind of brainwashing mumbo-jumbo. Trying to be an open-minded, solid friend, I tabled my skepticism and went along.

The Silva Method turned out to be an incredibly practical and useful skill—right up there with driving and walking. I learned how to "tune out" and focus before presentations, important telephone calls, meetings—even amid hordes of people.

I Do It Because It Works

Meditation and visualization got me through crippling stage fright when I was supposed to do a live TV program, before an audience, for a solid hour without notes or even a clock in the studio. Basically, it was a training module I had facilitated hundreds of times for corporations. Yet somehow, this new TV prospect terrified me beyond description. I worked with Thea Lammers, my training coach, for a solid weekend and the words just wouldn't come—even though I had written books on the subject.

The morning of the program, before I got out of bed, I put myself in a totally relaxed state by using self-hypnosis principles and I visualized myself doing the program in exact detail.

In this meditative state, I actually felt myself becoming enthusiastic, experienced the pauses, saw the audience, heard the laughter, and took my cues from the introductory music for each segment of the show. When I brought myself out of the visualization process, I was soaked with perspiration. Yet when I walked on to the TV studio floor later that day, it was as though I'd done it all before. I knew what I was up against and I was relaxed and effective. That sold me. I've been advocating these skills to my coaching clients ever since.

The next chapter gives a detailed accounting of how I have combined meditation, self-hypnosis, and visualization to make my life work better.

To BUILD PEACE FOR YOUR OWN CLASS ACT, YOU NEED TO INCLUDE THESE BRICKS IN YOUR FOUNDATION:

- Tuning in
- Meditation
- Relaxation
- Stress control

CHAPTER 8

Einstein Had the Answer

"The intuitive mind is a sacred gift and the rational mind is a faithful servant. We have created a society that honors the servant and has forgotten the gift."

—Albert Einstein

We have become a world of humans *doing* instead of humans *being*; we work for material success no matter what the cost. Winning is equated with the highest return on investment possible, with lawyers working tirelessly to find yet another legal loophole through which more revenue can be squeezed. Ethics, morality, justice, and altruism are all too often admired publicly yet dismissed in the boardrooms and the backrooms in favor of portfolio-boosting tactics that are defended as following the letter of the law, if not the spirit.

We are led to believe that being "plugged in" requires a cell phone, pager, wireless laptop, Palm Pilot, broadband Internet connection, and 24-hour news and weather channels.

Yet financial success isn't synonymous with class. There are Class Acts at all levels of the economic ladder. Money simply cannot buy class. And while solid interpersonal skills are imperative, it takes far more than knowing which fork to use at a formal banquet to be a Class Act.

When I asked the clients, colleagues, and friends I admire most to share their most important lesson for this new millennium, nobody talked about acquiring more things, building their stock holdings, or spending more time

at the office. All but a few of them spoke of the spiritual beauty of living a civil, successful, and centered life: A CLASS ACT.

ANSWERS IN THE FORM OF A PRAYER

The more I listened, the more their responses seemed to form a collective prayer. So, with gratitude to the remarkable people in my life, here is what they shared and I share it with you as a checklist of lessons that, once learned, will provide the path for life as a Class Act:

Dear Lord / Higher Power / Spirit of the Universe / Creator / God / Force of Nature, help me to remember:

- to accept others for who and what they are, and how they add to my life.

- not to jump to conclusions or judge others by my preconceived notions.

- that good relationships give me and others roots of stability and wings of creativity.

- that my family comes before my job.

- to trust my intuition and my heart; they always will lead me home.

- that the people I like the least usually teach me the most.

- to praise in public and criticize in private.

- not to allow the pace of change to overwhelm my humanity.

- not to rush through the steps of my life, not matter how difficult, but to savor each one.

- that wealth has little to do with money, and that I cannot be poor if I am rich at heart.

- to help others realize their dreams; in doing so, I will realize mine.

- that I can make a big difference in this world by helping one person at a time.

- how much strength there is in humility.

- that young people's wisdom is important, and I can learn from it.

- that my failures should inspire me, not defeat me.

- that courage is what overcomes fear and that faith, not fear, lives in my heart.

- to appreciate the gift of robust health.

- that ignorance is not the same as innocence.

- that you really do catch more flies with honey than with vinegar. And the effort is always worth it in the end.

- that I can't always make people nice by being nicer to them, or fair by being fairer to them.

- to allow room in my heart and mind for others' opinions, experiences, and solutions.

- that the universe always will inflict its will; as the future is truly uncertain, the present becomes more precious, more immediate, more delicious.

- first and foremost, that kindness is the best currency, readily available and easy to dispense.

"Learn to be silent. Let your quiet mind listen and absorb."

—Pythagoras

"Slowing down reminds you that the journey is supposed to be fun."

—Anne Bancroft

A CLASS ACT WILL DEVELOP THROUGH THE PRACTICE OF PEACE, CONTEMPLATION, AND MEDITATION.

Part III

COMMUNICATING

CHAPTER 9

A Class Act Communicates Well

"Half the world is composed of people who have something to say and can't, and the other half who have nothing to say and keep on saying it."
—Robert Frost

Class Acts are effective communicators. Either intuitively or consciously, they understand the communications process. Most of us need to become more aware of it. Why? Poor communication causes more problems in relationships than anything else.

I have yet to meet anyone who could not stand to improve his or her communications skills. It's a lifelong process. What I have heard, time and again, are phrases like these:

- "If only he'd listen to what I'm saying."

- "She doesn't understand me."

- "I'm going to a company that will appreciate me."

- "I've just spent half an hour with the boss, and I haven't a clue what to do."

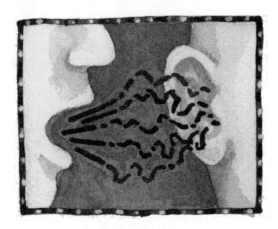

PERCEPTION

Situations, in and of themselves, are neutral. We make them either positive or negative, based on our own perceptions or reactions. Communication has little to do with truth and reality. It has to do with perception. For someone's perception of you is truth and reality to him or her, and they will judge you and treat you accordingly. And that perception is based on cultural background, value system, judgment, etc.

GET OFF TO A GOOD START

That first moment when someone calls you on the telephone or walks through your office door is crucial to both parties. Remember, what we say is not always what people hear. And what people hear is what controls the communication.

The first step toward effective communication is ensuring that what you say, how you say it, and how you look, send the same message. If even one of these three elements is out of synch, you are sending mixed messages.

We often think that once we've said something, we've communicated. No. All we've done is spoken out loud. Remember that communication has nothing to do with what is actually said but does have everything to do with what you think I said. Perception is more important than intention. What you hear is more important than what I say. For your perception is reality to you, and you will judge this experience and me according to your reality, not mine.

THE BASICS OF COMMUNICATING

We need to be interested in the other person, eager to hear what they have to say. In order to do that, we must:

Smile. This is the warm and genuine variety, not the pained, forced kind. Smile even if you're in a bad mood, because when someone smiles at us we automatically smile back! And how do we feel? Better!

Be open. From a posture point of view, having your arms uncrossed, hands visible and free to gesture communicates, "I want to hear you."

Lean forward. Tilt your head and neck slightly forward, as though you are straining to hear every word. It communicates, "I'm listening."

Make eye contact. Making eye contact, in American business, is essential. It communicates sincerity, interest, and honesty.

Offer assistance. "How may I help you?" "How can I assist you?" "Are there any questions you have that I might be able to answer for you?"

BODY LANGUAGE

A full 55 percent of the impression we make on others is based on how we appear, according to Albert Mehrabian, Ph.D., at UCLA. This appearance is called body language, and with it we can communicate as effectively as we do when speaking. Sometimes our body language says more about our communication message than the words we speak or the way we say those words.

THE ART OF LISTENING

The most important skill an expert communicator can demonstrate is listening, since about 75 percent of all oral communication is ignored, misunderstood, or forgotten! In order to be a skilled communicator, you should master the following skills:

TEN LISTENING SKILLS

1. Use Empathy vs. Sympathy

Verbally acknowledge how the other person feels instead of "knowing" how they feel: "I can see you're upset this happened," not "I know just how you feel." You cannot know how any other human being feels, so don't insult them by saying that you do.

2. Suspend Judgment

Don't think thoughts like "I know where they're going with this," "He says the same thing all the time," "They're going to ask for this or that." Unless you hear what is actually said, you won't know for sure. Focus on what the other person is saying, not on your reply.

3. Don't Interrupt

Often the purpose of our interrupting is to shorten a conversation. Actually, this action only serves to lengthen it. When any one of us is interrupted, our first thought is, "They haven't heard me . . . they don't understand." And our automatic human reaction is to begin to paraphrase and rephrase it. Allow the speaker enough time to state an issue or concern.

4. Tolerate Silence

It's okay for conversations to have gaps of silence. Most of us are uncomfortable with silence, so, what do we do? Talk! However, if you talk, you won't be listening.

5. Experience the Total Message

Hear the words, the voice, notice the attitude, and watch the body language for non-verbal messages in order to understand the total message.

6. Ask Open-Ended Questions

Open-ended questions promote conversation and, therefore, a better understanding. Begin questions with the following words: who, what, when, where, how, and tell me. Eliminate questions beginning with the word "why." *Why* tends to put the other person on the defensive.

7. Take Notes

Taking notes shows that you are listening and conveys to the receiver that you're committed to getting the problem solved, that you care.

8. Show That You're Listening

When speaking in person, or via teleconference, "listen" by making eye contact and leaning forward slightly. This will encourage the other participant(s) to "listen" to you.

9. Don't Do Anything Else

Listening requires total concentration. Nothing should be more important than what the speaker is saying. Don't be checking your e-mail during a telephone conversation, or if you must, make that clear to the person on the line so your action is not interpreted as not caring.

10. Remember Why Listening Is Important

Listening not only shows respect and consideration for another human being, but is the first step to truly understanding their concerns, needs, and wants.

GIVING NEGATIVE FEEDBACK IN A POSITIVE WAY

When giving someone negative feedback about their performance, behavior, dress, or another issue, we must try to be as objective and dispassionate as possible. Follow these rules and your confrontations should be far less explosive:

Examine your intention, your "purity of intent," or the "why," especially when you are giving someone negative feedback. Remember, there is a difference between disapproval, disagreement, and direction.

Give feedback when it can be "heard." Has the person just done something and is still feeling bad or guilty about it? Is now the time to voice your opinion, or might it be better to wait a bit until they are less ashamed or upset?

Focus feedback on the behavior, not the person. When anyone feels they are being judged, their immediate reaction is to become defensive. Once that happens, communication stops. Negative feedback shouldn't be personal.

Speak in terms of observable fact and observable behavior. Observable fact = what you know and can prove. Observable behavior = what you saw someone do, what you'd like to see someone do. This will take the judgment out of the conversation as much as is possible. It's about the behavior, not the person.

When communicating negative feelings or information, rely on words. When tensions are high and we have to communicate negative information or feelings, the safest way to do that is to show nothing non-verbally. The tone of our voices should be as though we're saying, "It's raining outside." Let the words carry the message.

Focus feedback on the future, not the past. In other words, don't throw up the past or blame by saying, for example, "You did the exact same thing last month!" When we blame, we judge; when we judge, the listener becomes defensive and shuts down.

Be specific, not general. Don't make blanket, general statements such as "You're always late." Instead, more productive feedback might be, "You've been late three times this week."

Check for understanding. We may think we've been clear, but has the message really been received? We need to check to ensure the other person has understood what we have said. Ask questions similar to "Just to make sure I was clear, would you mind restating what you heard?" "Could you summarize the points we talked about?"

Acknowledge. Acknowledge the other person's feelings toward your conversation. Acknowledge their openness to your comments. Acknowledge his or her good work in the past. As was discussed at the beginning, the reason for giving negative feedback is to provide direction, not to tear someone else down.

A CLASS ACT KNOWS THAT THE PERCEPTION OF THE RECEIVER OF THE MESSAGE MUST MATCH THE SENDER'S INTENTION.

CHAPTER 10

Introductions by a Class Act

"You cannot shake hands with a clenched fist."

—Golda Meir

There is absolutely no need to stumble, grope, stammer, or embarrass yourself in any way—ever again—when you are meeting or greeting people.

Remember, the meeting and the greeting set the stage for the ensuing relationship. If you've ever listened to someone being introduced skillfully, you will notice several things: the people doing the introducing take their time; they speak clearly, look each person in the eye, and are generous with their upbeat comments. Nothing gets garbled. They set the tone/stage for the ensuing relationship. The people being introduced bask in the attention and good will. They blossom. Yet, in all the training that I do, I observe more difficulties with introductions than with any other area apart from table manners.

So, let's start from the beginning and get a handle on the mechanics of meeting and greeting.

MEETINGS AND GREETINGS—THE MECHANICS

When Americans meet someone for the first time, they expect three gestures:

1. eye contact
2. a smile
3. a handshake

1. Eye contact can be challenging. If you are uncomfortable making eye contact you can fake it. Try this: instead of looking into someone's eyes, look at the space between their eyebrows. They won't be able to tell the difference, I guarantee it. Eventually you will work your way into the real thing.

2. Smile. Sometimes we get so caught up in thinking about what the other person is saying, or what we are about to say, that we forget to smile. Know that a smile is one of the few universally understood gestures—so use it! It warms up hearts and can completely alter the atmosphere.

3. Handshakes are a bit more difficult. People judge you by your handshake, so be sure that yours is firm and willing. The idea is to lock thumbs, so that you connect soft tissue to soft tissue, the "web" between our index finger and thumb. Shake firmly one or two times from the elbow. Remember, whoever gets the hand extended first controls the interchange. It's subtle yet true. Men should not worry about whether to extend a hand to a woman who might not proffer hers first—that rule no longer applies in business.

To make a good first impression, shake hands like you mean it. A University of Alabama study found that women with firmer handshakes were perceived by both men and women as being more extroverted, expressive, and open to new experiences than women with weaker handshakes. This contradicts the belief that people are uncomfortable around confident women, according to William F. Chaplin, Ph.D. "Giving a firm handshake may provide an effective initial form of self-promotion for women," he says.

When Not to Shake Hands:

1. If someone extends a hand to you at a party and your right hand is soiled in some way, perhaps from having just eaten some messy finger food at a cocktail party. Handle it like this: "You wouldn't want to shake my hand now," smile, and get a napkin to clean your fingers.
2. If you have a skin disease such as poison ivy. Tie a scarf over your hand in that case to indicate that your hand is out of commission. Extend your left hand to shake.

3. If you're wearing gloves. Etiquette mandates that we never shake hands with gloves on, whether indoors or outside.

4. If you have a bad cold, you might choose to decline a handshake by saying, "Forgive me for not shaking. I don't want to give you my cold." Never refuse a handshake, though. Should you shake someone's hand who has a cold, wash your hands ASAP, before touching food or your face. It's a good idea to carry small bottles of sanitizer.

TIME TO SPEAK

Now it's time to say something. I'll give you the formula, and I suggest that you commit it to memory. (Remember that good manners, like good judgment, are conspicuous only in their absence.)

Introduce a person of lesser authority to a person of greater authority, regardless of gender. That means you speak first to the person of greater authority. And this sounds like, "Mr./Ms. Greater Authority, may I present Mr./Ms. Lesser Authority."

Then you say something about each person as you introduce them; some nugget of information that will give them something to talk about when you've left the scene. This may sound like: "Mary Flannery, may I present Michael Kalisher. Michael is a litigator who specializes in environmental law. Mary is on the board of United Way in Philadelphia and is also a lobbyist in Washington." Look at each person as you address them. When you've made the introduction, both people shake hands.

Okay, you're probably thinking, "that sounds way too formal for anything I'd say." Fair enough. "May I present" is the most formal language you can use in an introduction. But think about it; it's also the most clear. So remember, give people their moment to shine. Ceremonies serve that purpose. If you aren't (yet) comfortable with such language, use, "this is" instead. So it would sound like, "Mr./Ms. Greater Authority, this is Mr./Ms. Lesser Authority."

Think of introductions as equations, balanced scales. Whatever you do on one side of the scales must be the same on the other side of the scales. Thus, you'd use both first and last names; as well as making sure that the info nuggets you provide are essentially the same. For example, you wouldn't say that so-and-so just won the Nobel Prize and so-and-so bakes great brownies. (In that case, the gracious move would be to say that one person bakes great brownies and the other eats them and forget about the Nobel Prize.)

And while we're talking about rank and authority, never forget that a client of any stature outranks any member of your firm, including the CEO. After all, who pays the bills?

HANDLING MISERABLE MOMENTS

1. *You cannot understand how to pronounce someone's name.* Simply say, "Would you say that again for me? I didn't get it right." All that says about you is that you care enough to get things right. That's a plus.
2. *Someone introduces you by the wrong name.* Just whisper your correct name into the introducer's ear. You don't want him or her to hear it from anyone else—that would be truly embarrassing.
3. *You'd like to break into a group of people who are chatting.* Just walk up to them, smile, and wait for a break in the conversation. Then hold out your hand to the person nearest you and introduce yourself. It's perfectly fine (and actually quite self-assured) to say something like, "I'm Mary Mitchell and I don't know anybody here. You looked like the most interesting group of guests, so I'm hoping you'll talk with me." No doubt they will welcome you and introduce themselves
4. *You want to introduce yourself to someone but don't know what to say.* After you've made eye contact, smiled, and extended your hand, tell the person your name. Then describe what you do rather than give your title. It gives the other person much more meat to develop into a conversation. For example, "I develop and implement all the community outreach programs for XYZ Company. We do a lot of work with inner-city schools to boost literacy."
5. *You only remember someone's first name when you're introducing.* Just use that! And only use first names for everyone. So it might sound like, "Hello, John. This is Paul from the purchasing department."
6. *You only remember someone's last name.* Good-naturedly exaggerate the introduction by saying, "Ah, Mr. Vandegrift" in a mock-formal manner.
7. *You only can recall the name of one of two people you're introducing.* Turn to the person whose name you forget and say, "I'd like to introduce Arthur Melito." He most likely will take the cue and introduce himself.

8. *You have to introduce two people and can't recall either name.* Say to the person who was the last to join you, "Hello, I don't know if you remember me from the Rotary luncheon? I'm Jane Darling." Chances are he or she will remember you and introduce herself/himself and the others.

9. *You cannot recall the name of someone you've spoken with before.* Say, "Please tell me your name again. My brain just froze. I remember so well talking with you at the coffee shop." Remember, everyone has blanked on names. We forgive others for mistakes we have made ourselves. By going straight for the solution, you aren't embarrassing anyone over the problem.

10. *You are "so bad at names" that going to any party is terrifying.* Tell yourself this very moment that, until today, you were bad at names. Put your energy into what you do want, not what you don't want. Here's one way I remember names. I make associations when I meet the person, in the course of the conversation. For example, I might say, "Is that Catharine with a 'K' or a 'C'?" Or, "Hello, Paul, that's my dad's name and I've always loved it." It is all a function of listening and paying attention. None of us is infallible—and we all can improve.

11. *You don't know whether to call someone by his or her first name.* When in doubt, don't. That's a pretty solid rule to live by, and it's especially true when someone outranks you. It's a sign of respect and an invitation for them to change the rules and request that you use a first name. If you're at a reception and everyone is a peer, use first names. Never, ever introduce yourself by an honorific—for example, "I'm Ms. Mitchell." If you're a young associate, call older people by their surnames. If you're a newcomer to a company, ask your senior colleagues privately, "What should I call you?"

REMEMBERING NAMES

Here's a technique that you can use to remember names that really works. When you have been introduced to someone, say the name aloud as soon as you hear it, again three minutes later, ten minutes later, and finally, an hour or two later. No matter when you see that person again, the name will come right back to you.

Speaking the name aloud imprints it on your brain.

TWELVE WAYS TO SABOTAGE YOURSELF

The easiest ways to sabotage yourself at a social gathering:

1. Not listening
2. Weak handshake
3. Negative body language
4. Smoking
5. Holding drink in right hand
6. Dressing down—removing jackets, loosening ties, etc.
7. Getting tipsy—too much booze
8. Invading personal space—standing too close
9. Loud, boisterous talking
10. Staying too late
11. Touching others beyond the handshake
12. Interrupting

A CLASS ACT KNOWS HOW TO COMMUNICATE WELL TO ALL TYPES OF PEOPLE IN ALL TYPES OF SITUATIONS.

CHAPTER 11

A Class Act Makes Conversation

"Eating words has never given me indigestion."

—Winston Churchill

lass Acts welcome the opportunity for conversation and understand the value of what is said as well as the value of what is not said. Class Acts know how to bring out the best in others. This story illustrates the point:

When my kid sister, Eileen, was 16, she visited me for lunch. We ran into Joe, a close friend of mine, and a much older gentleman, who joined us. They had not met before and after an hour, I saw my sibling in an entirely new light. She went from being this awkward teenager to an amusing, articulate, surprisingly informed young woman. What wizardry was this?

In fact, there was no magic. Only the gifts of undivided attention and intent listening that Joe lavished on her. Did they solve the problem of global hunger or world peace? No. Did they engage in high-minded intellectual discussions? Hardly. What they did was a perfect minuet of small talk, and in this case the gentleman led the dance.

FIRST IMPRESSIONS

Clients and friends ask me all the time, "What do I say to people when I meet them for the first time?"

I don't want you to feel any additional pressure, but the fact is that you only get one chance to make a first impression. Behind the question lies the real uncertainty: "What can I say to engage them so they think I'm interesting to talk with, so that they like me?" Notice all the "I's" in those sentences? That's a big clue.

If you want to be interesting to your conversation partners, be interested in them. If you really think about it, the people you consider artful conversationalists are most likely wonderful listeners. They know how to take their egos out of what is being said, how to be present, and how to be genuinely interested in the other person.

Let me paint you a picture. Most of us feel awkward making conversation because, while we're supposed to be paying attention to the other person, we're actually thinking about what to say next. And at the same time, we're giving ourselves a lot of negative self-talk that might sound like, "Why did I wear this outfit; it makes me look fat." Or, "My hair is a disaster today." Or, "I haven't a clue what to say here. Oh, God, she must think I'm really stupid." Imagine a movie camera focusing on you, like your third eye. You can take this to the bank—when that third eye is trained on you, you're bound to be a conversational dud.

On the other hand, turn that third eye/camera onto the other person and watch what happens. The gift of your time and attention showered on him or her will make the person blossom, I guarantee it. As that person relaxes and opens up, your own self-confidence gets a big boost. It never fails.

MAKING SMALL TALK

Small talk is a safety net. While, superficially, it has a very bad reputation, consider this: those first few moments provide us with valuable information about the other person through their enthusiasm, body language, and choice of words. Small talk is like a gentle dance—a first date—no commitments yet, only the possibility of a relationship. And in that first gentle dance there are no threatening, invasive gestures or words.

Make no mistake, small talk is crucial, because that's when we determine whether we want to take the relationship further.

It's worth practicing small talk. My dad used to force us to practice at dinner each night. I hated it. Now I am grateful for the experience. Our families are great research laboratories for these things. One thing I know is this: get good at small talk and you will be sought out for any party.

BECOME A GOOD LISTENER

Listening, truly listening, is the key that opens the door to the treasures of any relationship. Most of us say much more with what we don't articulate, and a real listener will understand. A listener hears. When we listen, the gift of our attention bestows value on the person who is speaking. It's a gift. It's the ultimate win-win. It's so easy to get it backwards, to spend all one's time and energy thinking about what we're going to say.

The noted Harvard scholar Charles Copeland was once approached by a student who asked: "Why are there no courses in conversation? Is there anything I can do to learn the art of conversation?" "Of course there is," answered Copeland, "and if you'll just listen, I'll tell you what it is." There ensued a long and uncomfortable silence which the student finally interrupted with: "Well, I'm listening." "You see," Copeland said triumphantly, "you're learning already."

Yes, listening takes some discipline and practice. Especially listening to one person at a time. Think about how demeaning it is when, mid-sentence, we see the other person's attention wander away, distracted by someone else's voice or presence. Then there's the challenge of being completely uninterested in what someone is saying. As my mentor puts it, "Politeness decrees that you must listen to be kind; intelligence decrees that you must listen to learn."

Above all, be yourself. If you're naturally reserved, don't try to be an extrovert. When you focus on the other person, authentically and genuinely, your personal style will win the day. Class Acts are authentic and embrace their personal strengths to bring out the best in others.

HERE ARE SOME WAYS TO GET A CONVERSATION GOING

1. **Ask an easy-to-answer question about something in your surroundings.** That might sound like, "What book are you reading?" The idea here is to fish for a bite—see if the other person seems willing to have a conversation. Or, suppose you're at a business conference, you can say, "What's for lunch today?" Another great conversation starter is to ask, "Who are your heroes?" It really grabs the other person's attention and the answer tells you about their values.

2. **Ask open-ended questions.** Once you've gotten a signal that the other person wants to talk, say something like, "What do you like to do when you're not working?" "What made you decide to get into this kind of work?" "How would you compare our city with where you lived before?" "What did you like best about your vacation?"

3. **Make a lighthearted comment about your surroundings,** and follow it up with a question. That might sound like, "Isn't this a glorious day? Autumns in this part of the country are just the best. Are you from this area?" The person might say yes and then you can ask what he or she likes most about it. If the answer is, "No, I'm from Ohio," you can ask, "What was it like growing up in the Midwest? What brought you here?" Even a subject as seemingly banal as the weather can be a good conversation tool. Just remember to keep the subject upbeat.

4. **Give a compliment and follow it up with a question.** That might sound like, "I learned a lot from your description of aviation mechanics in Pearl Harbor. Are you a World War II buff?" Everybody likes to be acknowledged and appreciated. Make sure your question is genuine and use the person's name if you know it.

5. **Introduce yourself and tell the other person something helpful or something you think he or she might find interesting.** That might sound like, "I overheard you saying how much you enjoy hiking. Are you aware of the local hiking club? I'm a mentor for young hikers and I'd be glad to share whatever information you might find helpful."

THE ANATOMY OF A CONVERSATIONALIST

Follow these simple guidelines and you will be well on your way to being an exceptional conversationalist. People who are good conversationalists:

- LIMIT "I" in their conversations and focus on "you."
- SPEAK clearly and simply, using good grammar and clean language.
- DON'T boast about themselves and their possessions or accomplishments.
- LET others change the topics they might have started.
- ARE upbeat and positive and make direct eye contact.
- AVOID depressing topics and malicious gossip.
- DEFEND innocent people and those who are not there to defend themselves.
- HAVE a good sense of humor yet don't try to be comedians.
- TELL only appropriate jokes that everyone can hear.
- RESPECT others' privacy and professionalism.
- ASK questions and listen to the answers.
- GIVE and accept compliments and praise graciously.
- LEARN to discuss topics that don't interest them.
- DON'T pretend to know foreign languages.
- DON'T make important statements unless they're sure of the facts.

- DON'T slap others on the back, take their arms, or engage in physical contact.

- WELCOME others into the group.

- BRING out the best in everyone.

HANDLING MISERABLE MOMENTS

1. **There is a long silence in the conversation.** Breathe. Know that it's not your fault and that there is a natural life to any topic. In addition, there is nothing wrong with appearing as if you're thinking! When this happens, it's time to change the subject, so do so. You might want to change your geographical location at that point, too. For example, "Have you seen the buffet yet? I think I'll meander over—want to join me?"

2. **The conversation gets dicey or invasive and you need to change the subject.** You are at a loss, feeling totally uninformed. Don't be afraid that you don't know something. Say something like, "I'm really not up on that at all. What do you find most compelling about it?" Or, "Why do you think it's so popular?" Then listen to the answers. Above all, don't try to bluff—it only will catch up with you.

3. **Someone asks what you do and you're unemployed or in a humble job.** Don't apologize or lie! You might say, "Right now I'm looking for a better situation. I was with XYZ Company until October, so I'm coaching tennis . . . tending bar . . . temping . . . for the time being." The good news is that today most of us respect and forgive lots of career transitions. Again, avoid the wisecrack approach—it only makes you appear scared and insecure. Self-deprecation makes others uncomfortable.

4. **Someone tells you very bad news on a highly personal level.** "My husband just told me he's leaving me." "My sister was just convicted of embezzlement and is going to prison." "I've just filed for bankruptcy." "My mother just died." "My son just came out of the closet." Caution: Do not blurt out the first thing that comes to mind. Breathe. Then say something like, "What a terrible thing to go through. This must be a difficult time for you. I am so sorry. What can I do to help?" Note: Do not make judgments or use this as an invitation to gossip. Instead, think of how the person must be feeling and respond to that.

Whether or not you happen to agree, no one can argue with how a person feels. So acknowledge the feelings without cynicism. Don't put yourself in the position of the messenger who gets shot. Your soon-to-be-divorced friend and spouse might reconcile—and you might lose a friend if you've labeled the spouse a lazy, good-for-nothing, cheating SOB. Above all, let the person talk and do not interrupt. Resist the urge to say too much, and keep what you learn to yourself

A CLASS ACT NEVER ASKS THESE QUESTIONS

It's surprisingly easy to go beyond the boundaries of good taste. Sometimes we are just impulsive; sometimes we genuinely want to know what's going on in someone's life. Nonetheless, don't ask people:

- (over the age of 30) their age. (Don't try to be slick and try to figure out their age by asking what year they graduated from college.)

- how much they weigh.

- why they don't drink alcohol.

- whether they have had cosmetic surgery.

- about a past prison experience.

- how much money they make.

- whether they are terminally ill—and this includes family members.

- about confidential business matters.

- why their spouse or significant other is not at the party.

- about the status of their marriage, or terms of their divorce.

- about their sex life.

- why they left their company.

- whether they are undergoing psychotherapy or have done so.

- particularly women, about why they aren't married, don't have children, or have so many children.

- about how they handle tax shelters and deductions.

- about the price of their house or the size of their mortgage.

- for details of their medical, legal, vacation, or other unusual expenses.

- what kind of deal they got on anything, especially luxury items.

A CLASS ACT IS A MASTER OF CONVERSATION.

CHAPTER 12

A Class Act Knows How to Disagree Without Being Disagreeable

"Nobody ever listens themselves out of a job."

—Anonymous

Conflict resolution boils down to preventing a situation from getting worse, soothing ruffled egos so as to avoid a buildup of resentment, and reaching agreement on how to move forward to get things done.

When someone is complaining to you about a situation or lodging a protest of some kind, it is best to:

- Listen attentively without interrupting.

- Take notes.

- Call them by name.

- Agree with their right to complain.

- Don't take their anger personally.

- Thank them for bringing it to your attention.

- Acknowledge their emotions.

- Repeat what they said back to them to make sure you understood.

- Apologize if their complaint or protest is valid.

· Take action to correct the problem.

Disagreeing is part of life; a big part. That is why it's so important to master the skills to disagree effectively. Some words of warning: whether you're disagreeing with your boss, a colleague, or a subordinate, always choose which battle you really want to fight and whether or not it's worth fighting. To help you make this decision, be sure to consider the timing, the location, the relative importance of the issue, how far you're prepared to go to win, and the consequences of losing.

One friend passed along these words that have helped me, and I am passing them along to you. Making money is not the point here—it's deciding whether or not to fight.

Does this absolutely need to be said?

Does this absolutely need to be said now?

Does this absolutely need to be said now, by me?

If your answer is yes to *all three questions*—a rare occurrence—proceed.

ALWAYS DISAGREE IN PRIVATE, IF POSSIBLE

If you disagree in front of others, chances are you will derail the interchange. Public criticism is the most ineffective way to hold a conversation, much less change someone's mind or behavior. When we are criticized in front of others, we are unable to hear the criticism and we mentally build our defense.

Should a dispute come on in public, deflect it whenever possible by saying something like, "I'd like to think about that for a bit and speak with you later. This really is not the best place for the discussion."

DON'T LET YOUR TONE OF VOICE BETRAY YOU

Learn this essential skill: say, "It's raining outside." It is likely that you can make that statement with little or no emotion in your voice. That's the same tone of voice you need to employ when speaking the lines in the previous paragraph. Otherwise, you will come off as a bully or a whiner. It takes practice. It can be done.

Remember that our reactions to any situations will usually determine the outcome. We instigate the reaction in others, and usually do so subconsciously. Never forget your own power to communicate.

FAIR-FIGHTING TIPS

These "Fair-Fighting Tips" should help you improve and clarify your message when you find yourself in a confrontational situation.

1. Use "I" Language

An "I" statement sounds like, "I've been doing this for so long that I might not have been clear," instead of, "You misunderstood what I was trying to say."

"I" language is the best language to use because it doesn't allow for the build-up of defenses. Using the word "you," however, will most assuredly cause someone to become defensive.

Whenever we think we are being judged, our automatic human reaction is to become defensive. The moment we become defensive, communication stops. The other person stops listening because they are building their defense.

2. No "Zinging"

Many of us think a little, friendly "zing" is harmless. It's not and it's not fair fighting. Comments like, "Hey, I like your hair today. Did you wash it?" What happens when someone zings us? We zing back, and so on and so on.

One of the leading indicators of underlying negativity or conflict within a social structure or work environment is increased sarcasm. Perhaps you've heard the phrase, "innocent, harmless sarcasm"? The word "sarcasm" has its root in a Greek word that means "to rip and tear flesh"! What is innocent or harmless about that?

3. Don't Chase Rabbits

In other words, stick to the topic at hand. Generally, when someone chases rabbits, our initial reaction is confusion. Confusion leads to impatience. Impatience leads to resentment. By not sticking to the point, you create a negative emotional response in others.

4. Don't Interrupt

Mom was right! It's not only rude, it creates the opposite of what we want to achieve. When we interrupt, we generally think we will end or shorten the conversation. In fact, the opposite is true. When any of us are interrupted, our first reaction is to think, "They didn't hear me." Or, "They don't understand."

And our automatic, human reaction is to begin to paraphrase and restate ourselves, thereby lengthening the conversation. Let people say what they need and want to say, fully. If you do that, and people begin to paraphrase themselves, going on and on, then you should employ the next tip. (See Chapter 36 for more tips on conversation.)

5. Restate What You Heard

Say something like, "If I've understood you correctly, you feel the problem is thus-and-such, and I felt it was so-and-so. Is that correct?"

If we restate the message correctly, the other person's reaction most often will be, "Good! I have been understood." Then you can move on to the next issue.

6. Ask Questions That Will Clarify, Not Judge

Asking questions is the best way to understand another human being's actions. But in order to get the answers you want, you must know how to ask the question. For instance, whenever someone asks me, "why?" I want to revert to five-year-old behavior and say (hands on hips), "because!"

"Why" puts people on the defensive, and we know that defensiveness stops conversation rather than fosters it. Use the words—who, what, when, where, and how—to begin questions. (See Chapter 11 for more tips on asking questions).

7. Stay in Today, Not Yesterday

When we talk about the past, we bring up past conflicts or point fingers. Blaming is a judgment that invites defensive behavior from the other person, effectively ending all communication. If actions of the past must be discussed, *refer* to it; don't throw it up in anyone's face, like couples tend to do in the heat of an argument. Talk about today, the present, and the behavior you see. Talk about the future and the type of behavior you would like to see.

A CLASS ACT WILL PRACTICE THESE PRINCIPLES

These principles work. Just as with everything else, we need to practice them for about a month before they become habit. And while most likely they are merely reminders of what you already know, ask yourself, "Do I practice them?"

As one of my favorite teachers said, "We all know what to do. Successful, effective people do what they know."

A CLASS ACT IS A MASTER OF CIVILIZED, RESPECTFUL AGREEMENT AND DISAGREEMENT.

CHAPTER 13

A Class Act Knows How to Use All Telephones

"This 'telephone' has too many shortcomings to be seriously considered as a means of communication. The device is inherently of no value to us."
—Western Union internal memo, 1876

I t is estimated that more than seventy-five percent of all business gets done by telephone. The way you use a telephone in all forms—cell phone, satellite phone, pager, teleconference hub, or the headset and microphone of your personal computer—can speak volumes about whether you are a civil, centered, and successful businessperson.

CLASS ACTS KNOW AND USE TELEPHONE BASICS

Many very smart people make inexcusable mistakes when using the telephone. Here are the most popular mistakes and how not to make them.

Identify Yourself

In the business world, callers must begin by completely identifying themselves, giving first name, last name, and company. (This holds true even for inter-office calls, particularly in large companies.) Unless the other person is a friend or relative, say "Hello" instead of "Hi."

Place Your Own Calls

Place your own calls, whenever possible. It is annoying to pick up the telephone and be told to "hold for Mr. Brewster." The underlying, if unintended, message is that Mr. Brewster thinks his time is more valuable than yours. He can't take time to dial your number, yet he expects you to wait until he gets on the line. Getting in touch this way can mean that your conversation will begin in an atmosphere of hostility.

Be Clear

Vocal quality is the focal point of any telephone conversation. Speak clearly and think about the tone of your voice. (Yes, a smile can be "heard" over the telephone.) Maintain a constant distance from the mouthpiece. Don't engage in non-verbal communications with someone in the room—smiling, grimacing, etc. Don't chew. If you sneeze or cough, apologize.

Hold On

The person you are speaking with always has precedence over a ringing telephone or the interruption of a call-waiting tone. If possible, it is much better to have someone or some machine pick up the second line. If it is not possible, don't just reach for the "hold" button.

Ask. It's not good enough to just say, "Please hold." Ask if they mind being put on hold, wait for their response, and thank them for agreeing to wait. Many people find the very word "hold" annoying. Consider using these alternatives:

- "Would you mind waiting for one moment?"
- "One moment please."
- "Please stand by."
- "I'll check that out for you."

Be brief. Never keep someone on hold for more than one minute.

Warning. If the call comes a few minutes before a meeting begins or just as you are preparing to leave the office for an appointment, explain and ask if you can return the call at a more convenient time. If you are expecting a call you can't afford to miss, explain that, too. "I might have to break this off and call back because I'm expecting a call from a client I've been trying to reach all week."

Hang up. If you are the one on hold, it is perfectly acceptable to hang up after a minute or so. In fact, it may not be good strategy to let the other person think you have nothing better to do than sit there with a silent telephone to your ear.

Voice Mail

Voice mail may be annoying, but is a valuable tool that is a permanent part of the business universe.

Recording a Friendly Voice mail Greeting

Your answering greeting should be brief and provide some choices (the fewer the better). After you identify yourself, give the choices:

- Leave a message

- Call another extension

- Hold for the receptionist

Longer messages may be required by circumstances:

"Hello, this is Jackson Bartlett. I will be traveling today, Friday, and will not be able to return calls until after 7 P.M., Eastern time. Please leave your name, telephone number, including the area code, and a brief message."

If you are going to be out of town, you may want to say that you will be at the Hotel Bel-Air all week, giving the telephone and fax numbers. If you are traveling with a laptop, add that you can be reached by e-mail.

Before you record your greeting:

- Adjust your system so that it will pick up after four rings, which seems to be the unofficial standard.

- Write out what you are going to say, and practice it once or twice.

- Briefer is better. Start by giving your name or your telephone number so people will know if they have reached the right person. End with "leave a message." You don't need to state the obvious by saying, "I am either out of the office or unable to answer the telephone right now."

- Unless you are a musician or a professional comic, stay away from sound effects, gimmicks, and jokes.

Your Call

If you are the caller:

- Be prepared to speak promptly whether the telephone is answered by a person or a machine.

- Once you hear the beep, leave a message even if you dialed a wrong number. You don't have to identify yourself: "Sorry. I dialed the wrong number."

- Give your full name and affiliation and your telephone number up front, so that the receiver doesn't have to replay the whole message to get the number.

- Say, briefly, why you are calling. This is especially important if the call concerns a time-constrained matter. "I need to speak with you prior to tomorrow's auction."

- Leave your complete telephone (and/or beeper) number slowly, pausing between the area code and the local number. Leave your number even if the other person has the number.

- Say when you can be reached.

- Just hang up. You don't say goodbye to a person you haven't talked with. Don't say things like you are sorry you missed the person, or that it's the second time you called.

- Don't leave multiple messages. It is unnecessary and annoying to leave a message at 10 A.M. and call back with the same message at noon.

Caution:

Don't use voice mail as a way to avoid speaking with someone. If you make your callbacks during lunch hour or after office hours, the other person will have little trouble seeing through your ruse. Most voice-mail systems state the time of the call.

On the other hand, there are situations in which the call must be made during off hours. In that case, you can say, "I know you're not in the office right now, but I'm headed out to the airport and thought you should know. . . ."

Phone Tag

The best way to avoid getting on this irritating merry-go-round is to leave specific, but brief, messages. If you are calling to find out what time the meeting begins, say so and add, "If I'm not at my desk, please leave the time on my tape."

If you are calling simply to convey information, be prepared to leave it on the answering machine tape with, "If you have any questions, call me back. Otherwise, I'll see you there."

Another way to avoid phone tag, and thereby make the world a better place, is to say, "I'll be at this number until five o'clock. After six, I'll be at 123-1234."

It's good manners to return calls as promptly as possible. If there is a delay in returning the call, explain the reason for the delay when you finally do return the call.

Call Waiting Annoys

If you absolutely need this service, accept the fact that you will be annoying people who are already on the phone when the call-waiting signal kicks in. If possible, wait until you are speaking and interrupt yourself, and not the other person, to say, "Can you hold on a second?" And listen to the response before you click over to the other call. The first caller then has the option to say, "No. Call me back."

After you switch over, get the second caller's number, promise to call, and return as promptly as possible to the first caller. Remember, the person already on the line has priority, except in the case of an emergency.

Speaker Phones

This is a "convenience" that should be avoided whenever possible. People have a tendency to yell into them and, no matter what they do, the sound quality is never great. If you must use a speaker phone:

- Never begin a conversation on the speaker. Ask if you can switch over to the speaker and explain why. "Jerry McCarthy will be working with us on this project, and I would like him to hear this."

- Identify every person in the room.

- Only one person should speak at a time, and that person should move closer to the phone. Speakers should identify themselves each time because the instrument distorts voices.

- Sidebar conversations should be avoided.

- If someone has to leave during the call, he should say so.

CELL PHONES

Remember telephone "booths"? They were created with the idea that only the person you were calling should hear what you were saying. That's still a useful concept to keep in mind when using your cell phone.

The Bliss of a Quiet Car

On a recent trip to Washington, D.C., I traveled in an Amtrak "quiet car." It was bliss. No cell phones allowed. Fellow passengers also respected each others' space in every possible way. Clearly, this was the most civilized travel experience I've had in a long time. Like all technology, cell phones are glorious. Look at how much safer they've made us feel. Parents, siblings, and children breathe easier knowing they aren't far from each other. Cell phones bring us peace of mind when some detail of our job needs attention, or refining, or confirming. They also bring us joy when we are able to congratulate someone spontaneously or describe a sunset to someone we love who is far away. Yet in their glory lies their misfortune. A telephone call will almost always be an interruption, an intrusion. Cell phones make it possible to intrude into every single area of our lives and that is not a good and glorious thing.

Showing respect for others' time and space is something we should all practice. We need to keep in mind the telephone's power for disruption and be sensitive to that. By the way, there was not one empty seat in the "quiet car."

Cell-Phone Rules

· Use your cell phone in public only in an emergency.

· If you are not expecting an urgent call, turn the cell phone off during business meetings, at social gatherings, in restaurants, and at the theater. In these situations, rely on your beeper, and have the beeper set on vibrate.

· If you absolutely must keep your cell phone on during a meeting, explain in advance.

· If you must make a call at a social gathering or at a restaurant, excuse yourself and find a reasonably private place in which to make the call.

· If you must speak while others are near, speak softly. Your conversation may be fascinating to you, but it's intrusive for others.

- Don't ask to borrow a cell phone unless it is a matter of urgency. Then, use it sparingly. Remember that the lender is paying for the call, and if the person receiving the call is on a cell phone, they are also charged for air time.

In the Car

If you use your cell phone while driving, pull over, and take the few minutes you need to dial your call. People who dial and drive develop a worthy reputation for reckless and dangerous behavior. If you must talk on the phone while driving, invest in a hands-free device.

TELECONFERENCING

Teleconferencing—instant, personal, global, and intimidating—is putting the formality back into meetings and creating a whole new field of business etiquette. This gives you the opportunity to put on an inter-company, inter-city, international display of bad manners unless you are aware of the new rules: it's not only how you look, but where you look. It's gestures, expressions, voice, and camera awareness.

If teleconferencing hasn't reached you yet, it will sooner than later. The cost of travel and the increasing sophistication of the equipment have combined to make teleconferencing the wave of the future. You may need to prepare more carefully for a teleconference than for a traditional meeting. Since you won't be able to walk out of the room to get something you forgot and leave colleagues, clients, or anyone else at the other end staring at a blank screen until you return.

Dressing for the Camera

The camera can magnify or distort clothing and makeup. Bright tones and patterns will come across more intensely on the screen, and the camera may distort bright colors; reds may become glaring oranges, for example. Conservative grays and blues work best. A pale blue shirt is generally better than a white shirt, because large white areas (as well as bright colors) cause glare. When the camera compensates for glare, it make faces darker.

Women should resist the temptation to over apply makeup. Men should be freshly shaved to minimize five o'clock shadow. Jewelry should be low key, no dangling earrings or big, bright pins or brooches. Don't flash your Rolex. Dress should be more conservative than casual, particularly if meeting with people in or from Europe and Asia. Suits are more suitable than sweaters and shirtsleeves.

Meeting Rules

The usual rules for meeting manners apply, but with the important additions described below. You will find that teleconferencing requires even more formal behavior and consideration of others than in face-to-face meetings. Posture, always important, counts for even more in these circumstances.

Picture

Resist the temptation to look at the monitor while you are speaking. Instead look at and into the lens of the camera. The camera lens is the electronic equivalent of looking the other person in the eye. You can look at the monitor when the other person is speaking, but keep in mind that the other person sees you looking away from him when you shift your gaze to the monitor. Since the camera has no peripheral vision, keep your body within the range of the camera lens.

Sound

There may be a slight sound delay, particularly with overseas transmissions, so expect pauses and wait for them. Speak slowly and clearly in your normal tone of voice. If the people at the other end have trouble hearing you, they will let you know and you can raise the level of your voice a bit.

Only one person should speak at a time. If there is a team on hand at your end, elect a captain who will do most of the talking. Remember that faces will appear on the screen one by one, and you can't hand out business cards. Thus, under some conditions, name cards with dark, easy-to-read writing are appropriate.

Nobody in the meeting room should be holding side-bar conversations within range of the microphone. Remember, too, that interrupting, speaking too loudly, and broad gestures are exaggerated on camera.

A CLASS ACT PRACTICES TELEPHONE ETIQUETTE

- Learn proper telephone manners. Don't assume that you have good ones just because you use the telephone a lot.

- How you present yourself over the phone is as important as how you present yourself in person.

- Always begin by identifying yourself clearly and completely.

- The caller on the line has precedence over a ringing telephone.

- Never say, "I'll let you go now." The implication is that you are in charge of the conversation and are being generous in allowing the other person to hang up.

- Always check your voice mail before heading out to an appointment. The person you are expecting to meet may have called to cancel.

- Keep voice-mail messages as brief as possible, and forget about gimmicks and jokes.

- "Conveniences" such as call waiting and speaker phones should be used sparingly.

- Teleconferencing involves an entirely different set of meeting etiquette rules, involving not only how you look but where you look. You can't get away with little asides, nods, scratching, and other small diversions that may be overlooked at conventional meetings.

A CLASS ACT IS AN EFFECTIVE COMMUNICATOR IN ALL MEDIUMS.

CHAPTER 14

A Class Act Retains Humanity in Cyberspace

"The Internet allows long-distance conversations, but not handshakes."
—Economist Edward Leame

CYBERCHALLENGES: E-MAIL AND THE INTERNET

If you're afraid to call someone to discuss a sensitive subject and think that firing off a message via e-mail is the easy way out, think again.

E-mail is a flawed medium, because the sender often forgets that the e-message is not the last word; I am as guilty as anyone of using (abusing) it as a means of avoiding confrontation. I nearly tossed away someone near and dear to me because of a misunderstanding that was made worse by e-mail exchanges and could have been cleared up with a simple telephone call.

It's too easy to send off an incendiary salvo when others don't do what we want them to do. We might feel better for having let off steam, but the consequences can be pricey at best.

The bottom line is, pick up the telephone when you need to. E-mail will *never* provide you with the tone of voice or gestures that say so much in their absence. "Netiquette"'s primary rule is, if you wouldn't say it face-to-face, do not say it in cyberspace. (This is a classic example of the Asian proverb, "We teach what we want to learn.")

NETIQUETTE RULES

To be a class act in the business world, you must be adept at all means of communication. Flouting the rules of netiquette, whether through ignorance or deliberately, will damage your reputation just as surely as bad table manners or rude behavior during meetings. Some of the rules are obvious. Just because you may never see or ever meet those you deal with through the Internet, there is no justification for being rude. If you ask for information say, "please." If someone does you a favor or responds to a question, say "thank you."

Some users are deliberately rude. Don't play into their hands by responding with an angry tirade. It's a waste of time.

A good rule of thumb is to compose your e-mail, save it as a draft, then walk away from your computer for a short break. Go back and take a second look at the e-mail, and then hit the "Send" button.

ADDRESSING

Be just as careful about who you might be excluding as who you are including when you send an e-mail to a group of colleagues or clients. This is important even if you are not displaying all of the recipient's e-mail addresses, since it is so easy for someone to pass it along, asking: "Have you seen this?" People can become quite upset if you cut them out of the initial loop.

It is also poor form to display in the "To:" or "CC:" sections of the address the names and e-mail addresses of people outside your company who have not given you permission to give out their address. It is best to use the "BCC:" (for blind carbon copy) section if you are sending a general message, like a change of telephone number or business address, to dozens if not hundreds of people at the same time.

FORMATTING

Don't write entirely in upper or lower case when writing e-mail, a posted message, or a chat-room contribution. Although typing in all capital letters may be considered the equivalent of shouting, all-lower case is not exactly whispering, and both are annoying to read.

You will become a better and stronger writer if you resist the temptation to use capitals to emphasize a word. Look for ways to make the sentence or the context give emphasis to the word or phrase. Don't overuse exclamation points either. And never, I mean never, use "smiley faces" such as this :-), or other cute devices in formal business exchanges.

FLAMING

This covers all insulting, vulgar, and angry e-mails. People are often "flamed" because they have made a mistake, expressed a controversial opinion, or revealed ignorance of a subject another user holds dear. Flaming is a little like dressing someone down in public, calling someone a name, or starting an argument in a bar, except that you only risk your reputation and not a right to the jaw.

You can save yourself a lot of trouble and emotional involvement by simply deciding that you will leave flaming to more inflammatory personalities. It is more sensible and good training in real-world interpersonal relations to respond gently to errors, flawed arguments, and wrong-headed opinions. Just correct the error. You can say, "The trouble with your argument is . . . " Or "That may be your opinion, but I believe. . . ." People are more apt to read and remember such responses.

If you absolutely must flame, start with "FLAME ON" and end with "FLAME OFF" so that people can skip your outburst if they wish.

Of course, you may elect to spare people your angry retort by sending it directly to the e-mail box of the person who has offended your sensibilities. Taking the dispute to private e-mail makes a lot more sense than engaging in a flame war that others on your distribution list may find tedious at best and offensive at worst.

HOAXES

One of the most annoying aspects of the evolution of e-mail is the well-intentioned, but misdirected, distribution of hoaxes regarding viruses, taxes on Internet access, and urban legends. We all receive them, with the evidence that they have been sent to hundreds of people before us.

Most companies ban the distribution of such messages, leaving any formal notification to be done by the information-technology department.

Hoax e-mails are easy to spot, once you get the hang of them. For an introduction on how to spot a hoax, visit the Urban Legends and Folklore site (http://urbanlegends.about.com/) or Symantec's hoax center (http://www.symantec.com/avcenter/hoax.html).

SPAM

Spam is junk or inappropriate e-mail, including everything from advertisements to pyramid schemes, sent out to hundreds and thousands of users at a time. The best way to deal with it is to ignore it. Delete it and never forward it. If your company has set up a means of tracking e-mail spammers and cutting them off, notify your systems manager or other appropriate person when you receive spam. There is software that will filter out messages from known spammers.

Never pass along a chain letter through your business e-mail, even if the letter says failure to forward it will cause your leg to fall off.

SECURITY

Your computer is not a safe deposit box. Even if you are using encryption software, your secrets may not remain secret. Emptying your "recycle bin" does not guarantee that the file you have dumped is gone forever. Even reformatting your hard drive isn't enough to completely erase your data—someone with the right tools and skills can bring it all back to life.

PASSWORDS

Never give out your password to anyone. Don't look over the shoulder of someone logging on. They may think you are out to get their password. Don't use an obvious password, such as your name spelled backwards, your birthday, or your pet name for your spouse or partner.

The most secure password contains numbers, punctuation, and upper and lower case letters. If you think you might forget it, write it down and put it in a safe place. (Not your address book, please.)

There are quite a few password-storing and password-generating systems available that are either free or fairly inexpensive. One place to find them is at the Website ZDNet Downloads (http://hotfiles.zdnet.com).

COPYRIGHT

It is a violation of the law to use, copy, or forward copyrighted material, whether you are using a computer or a printing press. Don't assume that material is in the public domain because it does not have the little (c) on it.

Copyright is a form of protection provided by the laws of the United States to the authors of "original works." This protection gives the owner of the copyright the exclusive right to do, and to authorize others to do, the following:

- To reproduce (make copies) of the copyrighted work.

- To in any way alter any image they create. This includes adding to, taking parts from, and even converting the image to another format (which does alter the work).

- To distribute copies of the copyrighted work to the public.

- To display the copyrighted work publicly, which includes publishing it on a Web page.

It is illegal for anyone to violate any of the rights provided by the Copyright Act to the owner of a copyright. A lack of understanding of copyright laws can expose individuals and their companies to the risk of being on the losing end of expensive lawsuits.

WEB SURFING

Business people should not have to be warned that surfing the Web for personal reasons during company time is a bad idea. But it is easy to be drawn in when a colleague sends an e-mail saying, "Take a Look at This Site."

Many companies use software that blocks access to inappropriate sites and also tracks where employees have been on the Net. Act as if your boss is looking over your shoulder and you'll know which sites are business-related and which are wasting the company's time and money.

A CLASS ACT IS ALWAYS CIVIL AND FOLLOWS ALL OF THE RULES IN CYBERSPACE.

CHAPTER 15

A Class Act Knows the Power of Handwritten Notes

"Beneath the rule of men entirely great,
The pen is mightier than the sword."
　　　　　—Edward George Bulwer-Lytton, Richelieu

THE PEN IS MIGHTIER THAN THE PALM

Three men in the Jockey Club dining room were animatedly conversing when suddenly the talk broke, and they each reached into their pockets. Two produced their "spare brains"—one a Windows CE device and the other a Palm VII. The third man took out a bottle-green leather jotter and an S.T. Dupont fountain pen.

Two started tapping data onto their tiny screens, one with his thumbs and fingers in a contorted exercise and the other with a thin black stylus that seemed far too small for his hand. The third man elegantly and smoothly scribbled something on the cream-colored paper card. His presence was as arresting as it was understated in its quiet confidence.

So it goes in today's battle of personal styles. Do you opt for technology and speed? Are you driven to own the latest wireless "techno toy"? Or is an air of tranquil grace more compelling?

A WELL-WRITTEN LETTER HAS MAGICAL POWERS

For me, the pen is far mightier than the computer chip. A well-written letter on good stationery has powers no e-mail or computer printout can match. A handwritten letter is so much more than an instrument for conveying facts.

In business, its very appearance makes a statement about your organization. The letter's style and content also speak clearly to your qualities as a person and as a professional.

In your personal life, a letter can be a gift that pleases both the sender and the receiver. It is more personal than a telephone call and more intimate and touching than even a private conversation. To the recipient, a handwritten note on fine paper is so much more meaningful than an e-mail. (Do people print out e-mails and place them under their pillows or in their treasure chests?) The letter can become a keepsake or perhaps even part of a family's history.

The value we place on handwritten notes today may in part be a reaction to the lack of personal involvement in modern correspondence, which often takes its toll on the way we express ourselves. While the e-mail phenomenon has been a pivotal and undeniable advance in communications, it has underscored the need for a more personalized, lasting form of correspondence. Modern technology has turned love letters, thank-you notes, and even apologies into electronic greetings and virtual flower bouquets. In our haste to send off an e-mail, manners, emotion, and details are often neglected.

A RETURN TO THE OLD-FASHIONED

A growing population is making a return to old-fashioned written correspondence, and in so doing is reviving an art form that was on the brink of extinction. Witness the fact that Crane & Company, the most prestigious paper maker in North America and a supplier to Tiffany & Co., Cartier, and J. E. Caldwell & Co., has launched a chain of retail stores in wealthy communities. Crane, which has manufactured fine cotton papers and stationery for social and business correspondence since 1801, has never wavered from its strategy of providing the finest opportunity and tools for handwritten personal expression. Its latest strategy, to teach customers something every time they visit a Crane store and to encourage customers to write letters, is proving to be a masterstroke.

STATIONERY "WARDROBES"

Personal expression on paper has rarely enjoyed more breadth. Gone are the days when, for example, every well-bred woman used only fold-over notes in conservative colors, rather than flat, boldly colored stationery. Today, people are choosing to build up stationery "wardrobes," in colors and styles that have never been more vibrant. A practical stationery wardrobe includes three kinds—formal writing paper (engraved or plain), personal business stationery, and personal notepaper. Household informal stationery is another useful option, for notes to the mail carrier, FedEx delivery person, etc. At a minimum, a stationery wardrobe should consist of one type for jotting down quick notes and a more formal variety for writing letters.

Correspondence Cards

If I was limited to just one kind of stationery, it would have to be the correspondence card—a piece of heavy, stiff paper roughly six by four inches in size. It can be white or colored, and may include a defining border. The card can also be plain or engraved with a monogram, the name alone, or the name with address. This type of stationery is a most useful investment for both men and women, especially those in the corporate arena. A correspondence card can be used for any kind of short note, sending or replying to invitations, thank-you notes, etc. Men find these particularly useful and often have only this one stationery item for personal use. I go through hundreds of them each year, not just for notes, but also for gift enclosures and the occasional postcard (sans envelope).

Calling Cards

Calling cards enjoyed their heyday before World War I, when the woman of the house did the visiting. If the person being called upon was out, she left her husband's calling card and her own on a silver tray in the foyer of the home. Husbands only went along when the visit was to offer condolences, encourage the sick, or offer congratulations on the birth of a child, a major birthday, career triumph, and so on.

The use of calling cards went into decline as women became major contributors to the workforce and had less time to go visiting. Economic factors also contributed to their decline, as calling cards are relatively expensive since they must be engraved. Eventually, calling cards began to be used primarily as gift enclosures. Today, most people enclose informal notes with gifts because they provide more writing space. However, there is nothing more elegant than receiving a gift with a calling card enclosed. Janet Weiss, stationery department manager for J. E. Caldwell & Co., reports a brisk and encouraging upsurge in calling-card purchases.

I think this is to be expected in a world where the conveniences afforded by technology have also added to our isolation. Fine stationery is a sensual experience—the depth of the color, the clarity of the engraving, the lush texture of the paper itself. Using it is like wearing a fine garment—the touch, the style, and the color can make you feel vibrant, appealing, and happy.

SOME WRITING ADVICE

Give yourself permission to buy a fine fountain pen and a leather jotting notebook, to order informal and formal stationery with matching, engraved calling cards, and to start writing those long overdue letters to the friends, relatives, and colleagues who mean the most to you.

A Class Act knows that no piece of hardware, no electronic correspondence, can reach people the way a handwritten personal note or a real letter can.

CHAPTER 16

A Class Act Has No Fear of Public Speaking

"It usually takes more than three weeks to prepare a good impromptu speech."

—Mark Twain

Fear of public speaking or simply addressing a management superior can keep people stuck in dead-end jobs for decades. They would rather stay in an anonymous job that has lost its challenge than face the prospect of speaking to a group of people or trying to convince a manager that they should be transferred or promoted.

These same people have little trouble conversing with a colleague. But if that colleague is promoted to director or manager, they find they are unable to address that person without shaking with nervousness.

FEAR OF PUBLIC SPEAKING IS QUITE COMMON

Public speaking is the primary fear of the American people, ranking ahead of death. The comedian Jerry Seinfeld got it right when he said, "That means we'd rather be in the box than give the eulogy."

The best way to get over public-speaking anxiety or stage fright is to find a chapter of Toastmasters International, on the Internet at http://www.toastmasters.org, whose sole purpose is to provide a forum

for people to hone public speaking skills. The organization is open to everyone.

THE PHYSIOLOGY OF STAGE FRIGHT

The nervousness comes from the flight-or-fight syndrome. That's when the
body releases a surge of adrenaline, which causes blood to rush from the
internal organs into the muscles. Thus, the "shakes" are very real. The adrenaline rush causes the heart to beat faster, requiring more oxygen, so one has
to breathe harder. This sudden change of body chemistry causes the muscles to tense and shake. It's a response to fear that's been around since the
beginning of time. Today our bodies don't know that we're not facing a hungry lion or club-wielding rival. We are only talking to the boss. So what gives?

The fact is, whether we are competing in a race, running from a preda-
tor, or talking to a superior, our emotions are heavily invested in our performance. Usually, what we fear is not living up to some standard we have
set for ourselves. We fear a negative judgment in the eyes of parents, peers,
coaches, teachers, or bosses.

The only solution is to harness the adrenaline flow and use it to our advantage for peak performance. Great performers have learned how to do this
and you can, too.

You can also overcome stage fright by practicing visualization through
meditation, which is what I do. Once mastered, meditation is easy, although
it takes some practice at the beginning.

MEDITATION AND VISUALIZATION

To visualize through meditation, find a quiet spot where no one will disturb you. Sit with your spine straight. Both feet should be on the ground,
and your hips should be equally placed and balanced. Close your eyes and
breathe deeply for a few minutes. Inhale slowly for about ten seconds, making sure that the breath comes from your belly.

Imagine your belly as a bellows that expands and contracts as you
breathe. I learned how to do this while on the floor with my hands on my
abdomen. Truth is, it's a natural way to breathe. Just watch babies. They
haven't given in to stress yet, which causes us to breathe shallowly through

our lungs. Exhale slowly for about ten seconds and repeat the process for about three minutes to relax and center yourself.

You will feel your entire body relax. Once relaxed, picture yourself in the conversation with a member of upper management or your boss. Imagine every single detail: the room you're in, the lighting, what you are wearing, your body language. The more detail, the better. See yourself being more articulate than ever.

Practice this visualization daily. Gradually it will become less difficult and part of your routine preparation. I have practiced meditation and visualization for years, before going to parties, giving speeches, and doing television shows. The technique never has failed me. It won't fail you.

Once you master the technique, you'll also notice another benefit of meditation. In this world of screaming technology and assault by telephones, modems, fax machines, cell phones, car phones, and beepers, we all need sanctuary in order to be effective and focused. Meditation and visualization help us to create our own sanctuary.

AS A MEMBER OF THE AUDIENCE

It sounds simple: sit down and enjoy yourself. That should be all there is to it. But to be a successful businessperson who is also civil and serene, you need to know how to behave when you are facing the podium.

There's little worse, for the performers and those being entertained, than for a loutish audience member to be disruptive and disrespectful. A confrontation in the aisles would only make things worse, so don't follow through on that urge to shut down the heckler. Don't make a big deal of it, but don't stay silent either. Saying "It's difficult to hear the dialog," might be one way to handle it.

Most people know these things instinctually, but they bear repeating nonetheless.

1. Be on time. They will try not to show it, but most speakers are bothered by late arrivals. It knocks them off stride, interferes with their concentration, and disrupts whatever mood they were trying to build.
2. Be quiet. Turn off your cell phone and pager or set the ringer to vibrate. And make sure you don't have any reminder alarms set for your Palm or other PDA.

3. Don't slouch, yawn, stretch, grunt, sigh, or otherwise demonstrate signs—intentional or subconscious—that you may be bored.

4. Ask questions. Showing interest in the subject gives the speaker confidence.

5. Be complimentary. Try to say something nice to the speaker if you meet him or her afterwards. Reserve any negative comments that you may have for the privacy of your car or home.

A CLASS ACT DOES NOT FEAR SPEAKING IN PUBLIC AND APPRECIATES THE RESPONSIBILITIES OF AN AUDIENCE MEMBER. A CLASS ACT HAS A HEALTHY RESPECT FOR THEIR POSITIVE AND NEGATIVE POWER BOTH ON THE PODIUM AND AS A MEMBER OF THE AUDIENCE.

Part IV

LIFE SKILLS (ON AND OFF THE JOB)

CHAPTER 17

A Class Act is Healthy in Body and Mind

"Sometimes the best way to soothe the mind is to use the body."
—Art Carey

We keep our car running well by servicing it regularly—changing the oil every 3,000 miles, rotating the tires, following the manufacturer's guidelines, etc. We feel successful and confident arriving at an appointment in a clean, purring vehicle—a vehicle that reflects our respect for it.

Why, then, do we mistreat our bodies? How can we possibly expect ourselves to be confident and centered, and thus effective, when we eat and drink too much, deprive ourselves of sleep, and consider it exercise when we tap a computer keyboard or wield the TV remote control?

Ignore your body's needs and your mind will suffer. Stress will build up. You will be easily irritated and distracted. Quality of thought is directly related to our physical health. My niece Julia reminded me of this.

HONOR YOURSELF

"What's on your mind?" the doctor asked. The "doctor" was Julia, my niece, who had just turned six years old. I was the "patient," and we were playing make-believe, her favorite pastime.

"That's the trouble, doctor. There isn't anything on my mind. I haven't had any good ideas in a long, long time."

Her diagnosis: "I think you probably just aren't getting enough sleep. You should go to bed early at night and sleep until really late. And you need to drink really healthy drinks and eat really healthy foods—lots of water and juice, fruits and vegetables. You need to get more exercise, too."

SELF-RESPECT AND MAINTENANCE

Out of the mouths of babes, we hear the truth. "Dr." Julia's advice brought home a central message to me that none of us can afford to forget. Self-respect and being kind to ourselves come before all else. If we do not treat ourselves and our bodies with respect and kindness, how can we truly and genuinely be respectful and kind toward others?

Honor yourself. Eat healthy, drink healthy. Get enough sleep and exercise. Admittedly, practicing these lessons isn't easy. We live in a stressed-out, time-crunched, downsized, information-bombarded world. Finding the time to do for ourselves is difficult even though we know what to do. Ah, there's the rub! Successful people do what they know. It takes discipline and focus. And, if you don't treat yourself with kindness and respect, you may find that you are getting fewer and fewer good ideas, and need to have a consultation with Dr. Julia.

Dr. Julia, in her simple wisdom, knew what has been proven by science and medicine. The lesson to be learned is that successful people know what to do, but sometimes life gets too complicated and simple things (the things that work) get overlooked. Be sure you can see the forest through the trees.

DINING OUT WITH OTHERS

Dining with others is about the people—and the relationships—around the table. That's true whether the table bears celery sticks or a seven-course feast. Sharing sustenance is a gesture of companionship and generosity. Remember the opportunity to practice careful civility in this setting.

Be Prepared and Party Smart

The basics:

- Never go to a party hungry. Eat an apple, a piece of cheese, or some nuts, and drink a full glass of water before you head out.

- Watch your alcohol. I stopped drinking alcohol at parties a long time ago, when I realized it clouded my thinking and sullied my healthy resolve. It's easy to substitute sparkling water, a soft drink, or alcohol-free beer. If you wish, you can always toast your success back home later.

- Exercise or take a brisk walk around the block before the event to curb your appetite, ease your stress, and clear your head.

Dinner at the Boss's Home

The menu is baked brie in puff pastry, beef wellington, and chocolate mousse—not exactly health food. If you've done your homework and had your pre-party snack, hunger won't be gnawing away at your good judgment.

So you can nibble at your food, choosing the healthiest items in small portions, and sort of move the rest around on your plate to make it look like you've done the meal justice. This is not the moment to announce that you don't eat dead animals—or, for various other reasons, anything else on your plate. It's not fair or kind to rain on anybody else's parade by bringing up your virtuous diet.

Instead, focus on being a charming, upbeat guest. That's what will get you a repeat invitation—not whether you've cleaned your plate! Thank your hostess sincerely for the delicious meal, whether or not you ate much. Mounting a dinner party requires time, effort, and expense. Honor that.

Restaurants

It's easier to navigate the shoals of dieting in restaurants, where you have choices. But again, focus on the "wants" rather than the "won'ts."

That might sound like, "I'd love the salmon grilled dry, a baked potato, and green salad with oil and vinegar, please." "I'd love a white wine spritzer."

Or, "I'd love those wonderful mixed berries with whipped cream on the side, please."

Sometimes it's most gracious to avoid the word "no" altogether. When declining something, try: "I think I'll pass on that tonight, thanks." You're not making any judgment on the indulgence or the indulgers. It's just that you choose not to partake tonight.

Remember that you're embracing life's pleasures, not robbing yourself of them, with the goal of being the most civil person possible. The bottom line is you don't have to choose between healthy habits and good manners. Keep your spirit sparkling, your conversation warm and generous—and your opinions on yours and everyone else's diets to yourself. The reward will be the way you look and feel and the healthy confidence that you project. That should still give you plenty to chew on!

WORKING OUT AND SPORTSMANSHIP

Regular, strenuous exercise is essential to physical, mental, emotional, and spiritual health. It's also a great way to relieve the stress and tension of the job. It gets our thoughts reorganized by taking the focus off the "big deals" and putting it on the rhythm of a pumping heart.

And there's a direct benefit to participating in sports or activities outside the office, particularly with colleagues. You can demonstrate your strength of character when the competitive juices start to flow in an office softball or touch football game, a golf or tennis outing, or on one of those team-building wilderness adventure trips. Working out in groups is a terrific motivator, by keeping things from getting too dull and repetitive.

Women in particular should try to take advantage of the out-of-office camaraderie provided by sports or working out. Men have for years. Whether it's a friendly squash game or a jog around the park, business executives frequently use their common sports interests to network and get chummy with the boss. So don't forget: folks who sweat together do, indeed, bond.

Sportsmanship is etiquette with an application of perspiration. And sports etiquette is based largely on safety considerations. A good sportsman plays by the rules, gives opponents the benefit of the doubt, and is gracious in both victory and defeat.

Recreational sports should follow the same rules. We're all on the planet together and we need to watch out for each other. Perhaps our good examples will remind others to watch out for us.

EXERCISE PATHWAY ETIQUETTE

You don't need to join a club to get your exercise, and you might just find that a gang from your office is already heading outdoors at lunchtime to run, walk, skate, or bike. Most cities have their version of Philadelphia's Kelly Drive or New York's Central Park Reservoir. Just remember that there are inherent dangers in these seemingly safe (in the daytime, anyway) venues.

The Ten Commandments of Exercise Path Etiquette:

1. Thou shalt go single file. Strolling alongside a pal is great fun, but not when there's a lot of pathway traffic.
2. Thou shalt stay to the right. Mix and match is a good idea only when you're thinking about your wardrobe.
3. Thou shalt keep moving. Standing around, shooting the breeze with pals isn't done in the middle of path traffic. Move to the side.
4. Thou shalt leash thy dog. Runners, bikers, and skaters do not appreciate dogs on the loose.
5. Thou shalt leash thy little ones. Children should not be taught to ride a bike, scooter, or skate on a busy path.
6. Thou shalt muzzle thy Walkman. Listening to music is great relaxation while walking or running; just be sure to adjust the volume so you don't disturb others.
7. Thou shalt save thy Kodak moments. Save them for somewhere other than the middle of the path. Otherwise you may be taking a picture for your insurance adjustor.
8. Thou shalt skate forward. The middle of the path on a busy day is no time to practice skating backwards. Trust me.
9. Thou shalt give a backwards glance. If you must stop or slow down for any reason, make sure to look behind you.
10. Thou shalt drive carefully. If you drive to a parking lot adjacent to the path, turn in slowly and cautiously.

EXERCISE CLASS ETIQUETTE

The very fact that gym activities are so "me"-based makes courtesy an absolute necessity to minimize distractions and to promote safety. And since business colleagues and relationships follow you to the gym, it's another place where incivility can leave a bad impression as well as cause physical injury to you or to others.

Don't think it isn't necessary to exercise common sense and good manners in places where people exercise. When the fitness-minded get single-minded about their workouts, things can get pretty grim in the gym. People can lose all consideration for—or even awareness of—those around them. Maybe it's all those mirrors.

Ten Guidelines for Gym Goers:

1. Dress for success. The key words are clean and functional. Avoid anything that drapes or dangles. Wearing jewelry while working out is stupid. Scanty, sexy dressing is inappropriate, because it is distracting and embarrassing.

2. Bag your gym bag. Lock your gear in the dressing room. Somebody could trip over it, get tangled in the straps, and fall.

3. Don't be a drinking problem. Keep your water in an enclosed, unbreakable container. Don't even think about bringing food into class.

4. Keep it quiet. Exercise your jaws outside of class, not by talking during class. Loud grunts and moans are also unnecessary, as well as theatrical and distracting.

5. Rest those cell phones and beepers. They should be turned off or on silent mode.

6. Cleanliness is next to godliness. Marinated gym clothes (the kind you leave in the trunk of your car or your locker and then wear again) and grime are guaranteed to help you lose friends and transform your group activity into a solitary performance.

7. Keep your cool. So what if you always work out in the corner but someone beats you to it this time? Group classes operate on a democratic system. Let off your steam in the workout; not by lobbing nasty salvos at the "offender."

8. Forget flying solo. By definition, classes are group activities. So forget about doing your own routine; instead do your best to keep up with the class.
9. Don't crowd. Consider others' exercise space and don't crowd them.
10. Towel off. And not just yourself! Equipment should be wiped down, too.

Following these guidelines will guarantee a successful, safe, and enjoyable workout.

LOCKER-ROOM DIPLOMACY

If many of your colleagues, perhaps even your boss, are members of the same health club that you frequent, you can run into some awkward situations. Discomfort about baring some of our less flattering features is simply a matter of self-consciousness. No one expects you to look perfect. That's why you're at the gym in the first place—to get in shape. The best advice is to focus on yourself and the workout. Then you won't be obsessing about anybody else.

You may feel perfectly comfortable in your t-shirt and shorts in the cardio and weight rooms, but find it more than a bit embarrassing to meet your same-sex colleagues in the altogether in the locker room, particularly in the shower, steam room, or sauna. What do you say or do?

Self-consciousness is a trait most everyone but exhibitionists share to some degree. Trying to avoid your colleagues by timing your entrance or exit or, worse, by not showering at all, just won't work over the long haul. There isn't a person alive who is totally happy with their body. And embarrassment goes two ways. It just might be that your boss and co-workers got over theirs a while back—perhaps before aerobics classes were all the rage.

There are ways of being modest without seeming prudish, by using a towel as a cover-up. And you can simply be too polite to notice. Look directly into your colleagues eyes and nowhere else while speaking to them, and try to go about your business matter-of-factly.

A CLASS ACT KNOWS HOW TO STAY HEALTHY.

CHAPTER 18

A Class Act Knows What to Wear
and How to Wear It

*"Dress gives one the outward sign from which people can judge the
inward state of mind. One they can see . . . the other they cannot."*
—Queen Elizabeth II to the Prince of Wales

Appearances matter. The way we look influences the way others treat
us, respect us, value us. The first thing you need to know is that there
is no such thing as neutral clothing. Whatever you wear makes a statement
regardless of your intent.

A client brought this lesson home to me. Here is what happened:

"Listen, Mary, you have to understand that when we hire you, we pay
for the packaging, too," my client said when I reported my surprise that,
without fail, at least one of her colleagues mentioned my shoes by name
every single time I did a training program for them.

I had been doing an extensive training program for this multinational
company, working with a different group of new managers every week for
three months. Shortly before the program began, I'd had surgery on my
foot. The only shoes I could get on were either running shoes or Ferrag-
amo flats, the kind with the bows and logo on the toes. They flew in the
face of my "I don't wear labels on the outside" credo, but given the circumstances, they beat Nikes.

FASHION JUDGMENTS

Everything you wear represents a decision you have made and is a reflection of your good taste, your good sense, and your style. The first time people see you, they will react instantly to the way you are dressed, whether they realize it or not.

Socially, people may make a snap decision about your economic status or about whether you would be an interesting or agreeable person to know.

Professionally, their reaction can be even more harshly judgmental. If your attire is inappropriate, colleagues are apt to question whether you know the rules of the game and whether or not you can be or are likely to be a significant player. Your superiors are apt to conclude that the quality of your work will match the quality of your appearance. One senior partner in a client's law firm told me, "The people here just seem to perform better when they're in business uniform." I never forgot that.

Rather than telling you what to wear in terms of right and wrong, I believe in dressing in what is appropriate to a situation. So, when you are considering how to dress to make the most positive impression possible, ask yourself these questions.

- Who am I, and how do I want to be perceived?
- Where am I, and who are the people I want to impress favorably?
- Is my appearance showing the people with whom I'm associating the respect they deserve?

Dressing makes just as compelling a statement about others as it does about yourself.

Remember! If you don't know what to wear for a business or social occasion, call the host and find out, instead of indulging in a risky guessing game. We honor hosts by dressing appropriately and invite respect at the same time.

CLOTHES—THE MECHANICS

I believe that clothes do not make the man (or woman), but that they are a way of expressing one's values. Your appearance projects a clear picture of your mindset and values. People who present themselves extremely well are usually the ones who have the character, ability, consistency, persistence, and motivation to achieve their goals over the long haul.

The dollars we spend on clothes don't ensure taste. That comes through understanding color and fabric quality and how to match each garment we wear. Such understanding is a process that requires continuous awareness and, often, the assistance of a professional. It means trading up every time you spend a clothing dollar.

The Fit

My tailor complains that "men are only worried about their sleeve length and women are only worried about their hems." There is a lot more to consider.

Make friends with a good tailor. You can find one by asking around—ask the best-dressed people you know or salespeople in fine clothing stores. Go with the checklist below and ask a first-rate tailor how each part of a garment should fit.

· Shoulders

· Chest

· Collar

· Lapels

· Armholes

· Sleeves

· Trousers

· Skirts

Make sure, too, that you sit and bend in everything you try on before you purchase it And try on your potential purchases with the shoes you plan to wear with them.

QUALITY THROUGH AND THROUGH

Quality looks as good on the inside as it does on the outside (now there's a metaphor for life!). Here are some guidelines:

Seams should match and linings should hang evenly. The better a garment is made on the inside, the better it will wear.

Buttons should be securely sewn, with a stem between the button and the fabric, and should meet the buttonhole squarely. Colors should match perfectly.

Zippers should be neatly concealed and the same color as the fabric. They should work smoothly and flawlessly.

Jackets should fit squarely. Back vents and collars should lay flat and not pucker. Double-breasted jackets should have inside buttons and buttonholes to hold the line of the garment.

Leather items should be supple, the softer the leather, the better the quality.

Fabrics should be forgiving. Test fabrics by touching them. Compare them to other fabrics. Crush the fabric in your hand—that's right, give it a big crush. If the fabric springs back unharmed, it will serve you well.

CHOOSING WHAT TO WEAR

When in doubt, ask! Your red face over an inappropriate ensemble is not an attractive accessory! Here are some guidelines to help you decipher the language of fashion.

White Tie: This is as formal as it gets. If the event is a ball, the idea of balls, and therefore ball gowns, is that one dances. Thus, women should wear a floor-length ball gown, not a movement-limiting slinky number that is more appropriate for a formal dinner or cocktail party. Their shoes need to be dressy yet comfortable.

Men wear a black wool and silk tailcoat; a starched white shirtfront; white pique tie with a stiff wing collar; studs and cufflinks made of pearl, diamond or onyx; a white waistcoat; black silk hose and black patent leather pumps or dress oxfords; and white kid gloves.

Black Tie: This is still formal but less so. Men should wear a tuxedo with a white tuxedo shirt; braces; studs and cufflinks of silver, gold, or pearl; and black patent pumps or dress oxfords.

Women have more freedom of expression as long as they wear dressy attire. Pantsuits are fine, as are short or long dresses, together with dressy sandals or shoes and an evening bag.

Informal attire: Be careful! Informal does not mean casual. In fact, sometimes invitations will read "semi-formal" when they mean informal. An informal occasion means that men wear dark business suits, a white shirt, and a dark silk tie with a quiet pattern. Women are free to wear a dressy suit in an evening fabric such as brocade, silk, or velvet; a short cocktail dress; or a long skirt and top.

BASIC WARDROBE BUYING GUIDELINES—WOMEN

Suit, Pantsuit, or Dress: Invest in one of each, the best you can afford. Make sure they fit, don't show too much skin (navel, bare arms, cleavage) and are in some basic colors, so you can accessorize easily and creatively. Keep fabrics durable and avoid evening fabrics, such as lamé, as well as total synthetics. If you want to assert authority, wear black, white, cream, gray, red, or burgundy. Beige, navy, and teal convey dependability. Yellow, orange, warm reds, and lime green convey friendliness and warmth.

Navy blue blazer: Purchase a good one and have it tailored to fit. This will prove to be one of your best investments, because it will be your safety net—you can dress it up or down and always look professional, finished, and put together.

Shoes: Go for the classics with some zip. Black and taupe will work with just about every color. Make sure you can walk comfortably in them. Pumps or low-heeled shoes work best and, when made of fine leather and kept in good repair, will last and last. Follow the fashion trends with less expensive purchases that you won't feel guilty about discarding when they become outmoded next season.

Hosiery: Always wear hose to work. Summer's heat demands a different set of guidelines, which we'll discuss later in this chapter. Hosiery makes a look "finished." If you're wearing dark or colored hose, make sure there are no snags in them. One friend of mine buys dozens of black pantyhose at a time, the least expensive she can find to fit her, and then discards them as soon as they snag—or recycles them to wear under trousers. The effect? She always looks put together and well groomed.

Accessories: Take care! No wrinkles in scarves; no tarnished jewelry; no broken eyeglass frames; no tattered umbrellas with broken spines; no scratched and worn handbags, briefcases, or backpacks.

MEN'S BASIC WARDROBE

Men need at least three suits and a navy blue blazer. One suit should be dark blue or black pin-striped so it can also be used for informal occasions. Choose fabrics that are year-round in durability, and avoid excessively light or heavy ones, such as linen and heavy tweeds.

Ties (yes, they are coming back) should be silk, well-made, and coordinate with the fabric of your shirts. It's a good idea to purchase ties at the same time you purchase shirts.

Shoes should be of the finest quality you can afford. You'll need two pairs minimum. One pair should be lace-up dress shoes, such as wing-tips; another pair of slip-ons is fine. Above all, remember that shoes must be polished and in good repair—they always get noticed!

Shirts must be clean and pressed. Otherwise, you'll give the impression that your thinking is wrinkled, too. Straight and tabbed collars are a more formal shirt style. Button-down shirts and turtlenecks, with or without jackets, are good casual choices for work.

Accessories shouldn't be your weakest wardrobe link. Any leather goods—briefcases, belts, shoes—should be maintained and kept scratch-free. No stains or tears on overcoats or raincoats. Umbrellas should have spines intact and not be tattered. Shoes and belts should match in color. There should be no holes in socks, and no hairy legs should show above them—either wear longer socks or don't cross your legs.

BUSINESS CASUAL

Training magazine disclosed the following astonishing numbers: Nearly 75 percent of companies allow employees to wear casual attire at least once a week. Thirty percent of firms that permit casual attire report an increase in flirting among employees, 44 percent report increases in absenteeism or lateness, and almost 20 percent report increases in insubordination. It's easy to allow a casual dress attitude to spill over into a casual work ethic, so watch out. Keep in mind my client's comment that "Most of us, especially junior associates, perform better in uniform."

No-No's

Although every company's casual dress policy is different to some degree, most agree on these restrictions for both men and women:

- No denim
- No shirts without collars
- No sweaters without a jacket over them
- No short-sleeve shirts, except in summer and only with button-down collars
- No sockless feet or sneakers
- No tank tops
- No sweat/warm-up suits
- No long shirts with leggings
- No spandex
- Nothing you would wear to the gym, beach, park, or to clean the garage.

SUMMER STYLE AT WORK

As temperatures heat up, the signs of summer emerge: tiny tank tops, shorts, and flip-flops. But while some offices loosen their ties, figuratively speaking, this outfit is hardly acceptable for department meetings.

People often prefer to dress more comfortably during the summer than is even appropriate in a casual business environment. There is a fine line between looking professionally casual and comfortably sloppy.

Wearing appropriate attire is simply good manners, showing colleagues that you respect them and the workplace. But you can still easily pull together summer office wear, tailored to your work environment. Just follow these do's and don'ts for a foolproof look.

Do's

Do keep in mind the people you want to impress favorably, and look at what they're wearing. If your boss is a suit-and-tie guy year-round, you should follow his lead, no matter what your peers are wearing. But if your supervisor breaks out the khaki skirts and polo's come May, feel free to do the same.

Do choose fabrics that are lightweight, yet not transparent and not too form-fitting. Test fabrics by standing in front of a light or going outdoors and looking at them in the sun. Even holding a piece of fabric up to the light indoors can tell you just how revealing it will be. (Hint: Don't wear anything you can read through.)

Do layer for seamless outside-to-office comfort. Layering is just as important in summer as in winter. Scarves are great for protecting your neck and shoulders from air-conditioning drafts. A wrap or a light cardigan can professionalize a sleeveless look when you need to.

Do choose modest light-cotton sundresses. As long as dresses are pressed and don't show too much skin, they're great office options, say experts.

Do pay attention to footwear. Corporate norms are changing in regard to footwear. Some companies frown on open shoes of any kind. High-end executives generally wear sling-backs instead of mules.

Etiquette icon Letitia Baldrige has relaxed her view on open-toed shoes in the summer workplace and deems them appropriate for the relaxed office. "A good-looking pair of leather sandals with a low or medium heel can add a lot of style and pizzazz to office wear," she says.

Do keep toenails tidy. If your office allows open-toed shoes, feet must be clean. Toenails should be well shaped, and skin should be smooth and moisturized. If you enjoy pedicures and can afford them, visit the salon regularly. If not, simply use a pumice stone in the shower every morning to whittle calluses and file toenails weekly. As for chipped polish, take it off or touch it up.

Do check with human resources to see if there is a written dress code or informal rules all departments abide by.

Do remember that your smile is your best accessory. No matter how hot or in a hurry you are, remember to enjoy the season and smile. When you smile your eyes brighten and your mood lifts; it's your all-weather asset.

Don'ts

Don't skip the slip. Or the bra for that matter. Think of the scene in *Bridget Jones' Diary* when Bridget descends the office stairs in a transparent top that reveals a sexy bra. Her boss, Hugh Grant, had anything but professional regard for her at that moment. We're talking perceptions here. If you want to be taken seriously in the work arena, you can't appear that you're there to play. Ironically, summer clothing often requires more undergarments to accommodate the seasonal fluidity and sheerness of the fabrics.

If your undergarments are bound to show somehow, perhaps an outline under a sheer material, take care to keep them both in good repair and simple in design. Excessive laciness or bosom-showing bras can be distracting— and uncomfortable. Attractive cotton camisoles have worked well for me; they're cool and comfortable and come in a variety of attractive styles.

Don't wear your weekend clothes to work. That means no capri pants, no T-shirts, no spaghetti straps, no midriff-baring outfits, no spandex, and no shoes that can be worn for sports. Dress for the occasion. After all, you don't wear your best suit to the beach.

Don't bare unsightly arms. If your arms aren't in good shape, think again about going sleeveless. Instead, slip a light sweater over sleeveless dresses or employ overblouses in linen, cotton, or silk, or brightly-colored lightweight shawls. Cardigans, short-sleeved or three-quarter sleeved, are perfect seasonal solutions.

Don't forget about hosiery and socks. Grooming is all-important. If skin tone is blotchy and the skirt is fairly short, think about sandalfoot hose to even things out. But if you are in a conservative business such as banking, bare legs just don't work. Many hosiery lines have very sheer versions that circumvent the "foundation garment" feeling.

Don't let makeup melt on your face. Steamy sidewalks call for updated summer makeup. For summer, think sheer. Trade your foundation for tinted moisturizer, one that gives just a little coverage plus sunblock. Bronzers and self-tanners give a natural glow without damaging tanning. And remember sunblock. We get hit with UV rays even through the car window. Look for moisturizers that have at least an SPF (sun protection factor) of 15, so you start your day protected.

TIPS FOR PROFESSIONAL-LOOKING HAIR

A Yale University study of both men and women found a close correlation between bad-hair days and bad job performance—especially for women. A woman experiencing a bad hair day has lower self-esteem and feels "less smart and less capable of doing her job." An entire day's productivity can be destroyed, according to the study. So when one of your colleagues is having a bad hair day, be especially kind!

Everyone has had bad hair days. Unfortunately, when it comes to work, many women have bad hair years. "If your professional style isn't easy-care and adaptable, you lose," says New York City stylist Julien Farel. "Too many women walk into the salon with a picture of how they want to look," says the stylist, who has worked at the uptown Manhattan salon Frederick Fekkai Beaute de Provence. "They can walk out of the salon looking like the picture, but things fall apart when the technician isn't there the next morning to maintain it."

And hair is one of the most noticeable physical factors affecting others' opinions of us. Women who work very long hours or travel a lot need easily maintained hairstyles. Usually that translates into shorter, straighter hair, so they can do it quickly in the morning and not think about it again throughout the workday.

But does that mean the only career-minded solution is a boring pageboy? And what if your hair has a frizzy, mind-of-its-own bent? The best choices are elegant styles with soft lines. Don't be a slave to trends.

Rules for Hair

Here are some ways to get a handle on your hair so it says the best about you.

Hair always must be clean and well groomed. That means a trim every six to eight weeks. If your hair grows fast, make that every four to five weeks. Often, bang trims and other minor touch-ups are free or very inexpensive; ask your stylist. The debate about long vs. short continues. But these days, just as there is no hard-and-fast business dress code, the old rules about tumbling locks being too youthful or curly 'dos being too cutesy don't apply across the board. As long as hair is clean, isn't covering the face, and isn't shedding off the shoulders, it can look professional.

Match your style to the vibe of your workplace, no matter what your work level. At the Hotel Bel-Air in Los Angeles, *all* employees are required to look sophisticated and yet low-key (so they fit in but don't rival guests like Meg Ryan, Sir Anthony Hopkins, and Nancy Reagan). The director of human resources there, Antoinette Lara, tells employees, "Think about how you'd wear your hair at a club on a Saturday night. Then do the opposite when you come to work."

Avoid flashy hair accessories. Stick to tortoiseshell or natural colors and accessories like jaw clips that sweep up hair in back to keep it tidy. Tragically cute barrettes and pins in candy colors are better suited to club kids than professional women. And hair bands can project an air of inexperience or naiveté.

Keep the size of your face in mind when choosing a style. Big hairdos overwhelm small, fine-featured faces, but can provide balance to stronger, more pronounced features. Look for a style in proportion to the size of your head.

Keep up with your touch ups. Blonde hair with black roots only plays well in Hollywood. Everywhere else it just looks unkempt. Schedule touch-up appointments (usually every month or so) at the same time you get your hair bleached or colored.

Use these stylist-suggested tips for different lengths:

- Short, straight hair: Let it grow slightly so it's not spiky; be careful of cowlicks.

- Long, straight hair: Keep it especially clean and fresh; otherwise it tends to flatten and appear messy.

- Short, curly hair: Find the right products to keep it calm and smooth without greasing ringlets.

- Long, curly hair: Give hair a boost in height and volume, and keep it manageable by getting long layered cuts.

- Curly hair: Experiment with different products until you find the perfect one for you that controls fuzziness but emphasizes the waves. Just don't let curly hair do its own thing. It ends up looking overwhelmingly unprofessional.

A CLASS ACT REMEMBERS HOW TO DRESS AND GROOM APPROPRIATELY.

CHAPTER 19

A Class Act Is Generous of Spirit—
Gifts and Contributions

*"From what we get, we can make a living. What we give, however, makes
a life."*

—Arthur Ashe

The art of gift giving doesn't come as naturally as most of us would like to think. Thoughtfulness and generosity of spirit are the watchwords. If money were not an issue, it would seem that buying gifts would merely be a matter of taking the time to make a purchase. And if that were the case, you would not need to read any further. For gifts that warm the heart and touch the soul, we need to be observant, thoughtful, creative, generous of spirit, and somewhat organized.

GIVING GIFTS AND MAKING CONTRIBUTIONS

I have learned over and over that we must give whatever it is we want to receive. If we want more cooperation and respect, we must be cooperative and respectful. If success (however we define it) is our goal, then we should help others to succeed. If we want more joy, we must be more joyful. When we share the blessings of being kind, we create more and more to enjoy.

Give the true gifts of time and attention and don't dismiss people who you think can't help you "get to the top." Help them along, with a smile, a thank you, and a kind word. It will be returned to you in the end.

TIME AND ATTENTION

My building concierge, Bruce, said, "I wish all my clients were like you. You always say thank you and tell me that my work helps you out. It makes me feel good."

Yes, Bruce is being paid for his time and effort, as he should be. We all get paid for the work we do. Yet doesn't it make you feel good when someone offers you a heartfelt 'thank you'?

Whenever we say thank you, we change someone's life a little bit. This isn't about the time-honored traditions of thank you notes. It's not about etiquette. It's about being human. I read a study a while ago that concluded that American workers want acknowledgement of their efforts about as much as they want raises. We all want and need to know that we make a difference.

TO TITHE IS A PERSONAL AND PRIVATE CHOICE

When we give from our hearts, when we give in a spirit of love and compassion, we receive even more than we give. It's a basic law of successful living, powerful enough to change a life.

Perhaps you believe, as I do, that everything we have comes from a Higher Order, or God, however you define that. I have learned that when I put God first, through tithing, I am practicing a universal law of stewardship. At first, the idea of giving ten percent of my income to a source of spiritual satisfaction was incredible, impractical, and sounded mad. I was on-again, off-again with the practice for a while, until one day I just made up my mind that that year, I was going to tithe, no matter what. Although it wasn't easy, it opened the flow. No amount was too small—if I got a check for $20, I wrote a check for two. Some people give to their places of worship. Others give to land conservancies, schools, orchestras, public television. The idea is to give of your time, talent, and treasure, with no strings attached.

Since that day years ago, I have been blessed with a sense of well-being, and my income has risen.

OFFICE GIFTS: THE RULES

Gift-giving in the workplace calls for caution and judgment. It's better to keep gifts out of the office whenever you can. Gift-giving, particularly around the holidays, can turn into a popularity contest, resulting in hurt feelings or resentment.

No matter what the boss does, an employee is under no obligation to give gifts to superiors. In fact, doing this could be a bad idea: You could be labeled as an apple-polisher. In addition, bosses can become annoyed if they perceive this as an effort to push your relationship into an uncomfortable area.

The safest time to give a gift to a colleague is when something good—something unexpected—happens, such as a promotion, appointment to a corporate board, or winning an award. The gift should take a simple form; edible gifts like a gift basket of gourmet foods or chocolate, or a bottle of fine wine or champagne (but no hard liquor), are always safe and appropriate.

However, never send a gift of alcohol to a person's office. Most companies prohibit alcohol consumption on the job, and the mere presence of booze (even gift-wrapped) on somebody's desk looks unprofessional.

Give holiday gifts to your support staff. Depending on seniority, a gift may be modest or quite pricey. Give a gift certificate, for example, of $5 to $100 if you've been together from one year to three years; more if it's been longer. Make sure gift certificates are for places that reflect the receiver's taste, not yours—and never forget to hand-write a message of gratitude to accompany your gift.

E-GIFTS

A decade ago, my mother sent me a Fruit-of-the-Month Club selection for a major birthday. I was insulted. I remember thinking: "Gee, that took a lot of time and trouble to dial a telephone number and read the numbers off a credit card, didn't it?"

And ten years ago, I would have had plenty of company. Today, however, online retailing is booming amid our time-crunched lives. Selecting, purchasing, and sending gifts electronically can be a wonderful convenience, as long as you put some thinking into it.

Before placing the order, decide whether to have the gift sent to you, which will allow you to wrap and personalize it, or if you'd rather send it directly to the recipient. If you choose the latter, find a reputable, reliable e-tailer, one you've used previously or that friends have recommended. It's hard to go wrong shopping online at household names like Tiffany (www.tiffany.com), Brooks Brothers (www.brooksbrothers.com), L.L. Bean (www.llbean.com), and Williams-Sonoma (www.williams-sonoma.com), and the online mainstays Amazon.com and MuseumShop.com. If you decide to have the retailer send the item, request that it be gift-wrapped. Once you've ordered your gift selection, send a card or note telling the recipient that something is on its way. A friend recently sent me a note saying that "a taste of Wisconsin is on its way," and a week later a splendid assortment of cheeses arrived. It was a welcome and much-anticipated surprise.

RECYCLING GIFTS

"Recycled" gifts are a minefield, so resist the urge. We all do it, though. Nothing is wrong with the concept, as long as you make absolutely sure that all evidence of its recycling is removed before you re-give the gift. You don't want your recipient to discover an enclosure message intended for you.

It's also a good idea—a very good idea—to keep a log of gifts given and received. Red faces during the holidays should come from the weather, not gift-giving gaffes.

ALWAYS ADD A PERSONAL TOUCH

Gift certificates to restaurants, theaters, movies, sports events, and salons are always welcome. They may be the closest thing to getting someone what they really want. And it sure is easier for the recipient than exchanging a gift that perhaps they didn't want. Just present them with some panache. Try wrapping the certificate with unusual paper and ribbon and attaching a fresh flower, pinecone, or holly.

Come to think of it, wrap any gift with high-quality paper, along with bows and ribbons.

Must we give to someone who unexpectedly gives to us? No. It is better to accept the gift graciously ("What a great, wonderful surprise . . . you are just the best to remember me!") and surprise the giver later on.

There is no joy in obligatory gifts—at least for Americans. Cultural differences should be taken into consideration, however (See Chapter 36, "A Class Act Celebrates the Passages of Life").

TEN KEY QUESTIONS

I've learned to ask myself these ten questions when giving a gift:

1. Why am I giving it?
2. Is it sincere?
3. Am I giving it without strings attached?
4. Does it reflect the receiver's taste, not mine?
5. Is it too extravagant?
6. Is it kind? (No gag gifts that can hurt and fall flat)
7. Is it appropriate? (No candy for a dieter)
8. Can I present it in person?
9. Is it presented as beautifully as I can make it?
10. Do I feel good about giving it?

STUCK FOR GIFT IDEAS?

Here are some items that are almost always appreciated:

- Gourmet foods and candy
- Picture frames
- A bottle or case of wine or champagne
- A flowering plant
- A box of luxury notepaper with matching envelopes and a nice pen

- A gift certificate linked to the recipient's favorite sport, hobby, or art form.

- Tickets to a major sports event

- Tickets to a play, opera, or ballet

- Dinner or brunch for two in a nice restaurant

- Books or CDs

- A magazine subscription

- A silk scarf

Class Acts know:·

- That tithing is good for you

- Not to mix personal gifts and workplace gifts

A CLASS ACT KNOWS THAT THE THOUGHT IS MORE IMPORTANT THAN THE PRICE AND GIVES GENEROUSLY OF HIS TIME, SPIRIT, ATTENTION, AND WEALTH.

CHAPTER 20

A Class Act Knows the Difference Between Service and Servitude—Appropriate Tipping in the Business Environment

"The trouble with many people in the business world today is that they are thinking too hard about the dollar they are trying to make, and that is wrong from the start. I'll tell you, the person who has the idea of service in business will never have to worry about profits; the dollars are bound to come. The idea of service in business is the biggest guarantee of success a person can have."

—Henry Ford

Being of service in one's business, social, and family life has nothing to do with servility and everything to do with meeting a need, being of assistance, and helping people do what it is they need to do to get on with the business of living.

In this sense, we are all serving someone, whether we head a Fortune 500 company or shine shoes at Grand Central Station.

A LIFE LESSON

The moment I could get my working papers at 16, I got a job—the better to support my shoe addiction, I reasoned. I was a short-order cook and waitress in an ice cream store. I lived for tips, since my minimum-wage paycheck hardly made all my time there worth the effort.

In college I moved upscale and waited tables in a white-tablecloth steak house. My financial responsibilities expanded beyond shoes during college, and again I lived for tips.

Everybody should know how it feels to work for tips. The experience is a precious, humbling life lesson.

BE A GENEROUS TIPPER

From that background, I've learned to be a generous tipper. I've always been baffled by individuals who dicker over pennies. The difference between being "correct"—i.e., the fifteen to twenty percent—and being generous is relatively inconsequential.

In the years between college and today, I have learned two key life lessons. First, no one is alone, no one does anything truly by themselves. Second, when we give, we end up receiving so much more in return. Okay, so maybe it's not always an even exchange. The universe isn't like that. Still, in the big picture, it never fails.

PART OF YOUR TEAM

In my table-waiting days, I also learned that we "background people" are easy to forget and overlook. Whether they were grabbing a snack, treat, or quick lunch at the ice cream parlor where I worked, the customers were in a hurry yet uniformly thanked the staff for our service. Those thanks were reflected in our tips, too.

Later, though, when my customers were more "foreground people," it was disappointing to see how quickly their attention gave way to pride in paying large checks that impressed their clients, At the same time, they almost didn't notice us helping them to succeed in the background.

Lord knows, this is not an argument for the "Hi, I'm Mary, and I'll be your server today" interactive dining-cum-theater experience. It is an argument to remember that it's the ones in the background who make big contributions to people in the foreground. Yes, they are doing their jobs. The spotlight should not be on them—if anything, good service is unobtrusive.

Part of the Team

The point is, when people serve us they become part of our team. They are helping us do our job. They function as our employees for a short time, if you will. As human beings, they need—and deserve—to be acknowledged. As employees, they require acknowledgment and motivation. When you're working for minimum wage, there is no motivator like money, cash in the pocket. Think about how fondly you remember a boss who was generous with appreciation and money. Think about the lifelong good feelings you harbor for that person. Think about the goodwill you spread just by telling others how much you appreciate him or her.

At a purely practical level, it pays to tip generously. Your generosity will come back to you in even better service the next time. Most of us genuinely want to do the right thing. Most of us tip appropriately. I just ask you to consider the big picture and to enjoy being generous. (See also Chapter 19 on gift-giving).

GENERAL TIPPING GUIDELINES

Hotels

At an upscale, urban hotel:

- Doorman, from $2 to $10, depending on how much baggage he takes from your car or cab. Figure $2 per bag, and include odd items that might not be suitcases. After that, he gets a dollar or two, having supervised installing your bags from the car or cab.

- Bellmen who bring luggage to your room: at least $5 and up to $10.

- Room service: Check first to see that your gratuity is on the bill. Give the server an additional $5 in cash, since frequently they do not share equally in their tips.

- Valet: $5 to $10, depending on how much he assists you with dry cleaning, etc.

- Engineer and Technical Support: If someone comes to fix your heating or air-conditioning, or to help with your Internet connection, tip $5 to $10.

· Concierge: $20 if concierge obtained dinner reservations or theater tickets for you, arranged for plane reservations, etc., depending on the time and skill required.

· Housekeeper: $3 to $5 left on your pillow each morning.

· Valet parking attendant: $2 to $5 when they fetch your car.

· Taxi drivers should receive fifteen to twenty percent. I usually give a minimum of $5.

Restaurants

Never stiff a server. Even if you are displeased that you had to wait for your food, it might not have been the server's fault. Restaurants are orchestral operations and no individual who is polite and attentive should be penalized. General guidelines follow:

· Server: twenty percent of the bill, minus or including the tax.

· Bartenders should get twenty percent of the bar tab, paid on leaving the bar.

· Wine steward: Ten percent of the total wine bill. If you ordered exceptionally expensive wine, then figure $5 a bottle.

· Coat-check person gets a dollar or two per coat, as well as for boots and packages.

· Rest-room attendant gets a dollar; if she performs some special service, such as sewing a button on, then give her five dollars.

· Doorman who gets you a cab, five to ten dollars; if a waiter goes outside to do this, five dollars.

· Garage attendant who brings your car around gets $5.

· Buffet servers at an upscale restaurant's brunch have quite a bit of work; sometimes more than at a la carte meals, so tip as you would at a sit-down dinner.

- Fast-food servers deserve a couple of dollars for putting together your order at McDonalds or Burger King.

- Food delivery people deserve 15 to 20 percent of the bill. They use their own vehicles and must pay all those expenses.

- Tip buckets in coffee shops can be annoying. I usually put in 50 cents for a simple cup of coffee. If it's my neighborhood haunt, I put in a dollar or two every few days.

SALONS, PERSONAL SERVICE

Tipping does change from city to city. Here are some general guidelines:

- Manicure and pedicure: If your hands or feet are a mess, you should tip 25 percent; less if they are in relatively good shape.

- Facial: 20 percent

- Hair: If your stylist trims your bangs for free, tip $5 in a mid-priced salon and more in a deluxe salon. When you have a special "do" that requires more time and effort, tip an extra five percent.

- Massage: The going rate for massage therapists is 15 to 20 percent.

REMEMBER THE HOLIDAYS

Keeping in mind that the word tip is actually an acronym for "To Insure Promptness," here are some holiday tipping guidelines for a big-city business person.

- Doormen: a crisp $20 bill in a card with a note.

- Maitre d' at your favorite business dining spot: a $50 note.

- Garage supervisor: $100 in an envelope, to distribute among the staff.

- Personal trainer: One week's compensation. For example, if you train with a trainer once a week at $50 per week, then give $50.

- Club personnel: Contribute $150 to every private club of which you are a member; increase that if you use the club facilities frequently.

- Delivery services: If you have a regular service provider, tip him or her $10 each month if they make lots of deliveries. Otherwise, $50 at the holidays. Some delivery services are not permitted to accept tips or gifts of cash. In that case, send a big box of holiday treats to the office that services your area.

A CLASS ACT TIPS APPROPRIATELY AND GENEROUSLY TO ACKNOWLEDGE SERVICES RECEIVED.

Part V

OFFICE OPPORTUNITIES AND MINEFIELDS

CHAPTER 21

A Class Act Is a Model of Consistency, Compassion, and Civility

"And what I've learned is not to believe in magical leaders any more; that character and compassion are more important than ideology; and that even if it's absurd to think you can change things, it's even more absurd to think that it's foolish and unimportant to try."

—Peter C. Newman,
Canadian author and political columnist.

When I was a child, a plumber came into our home to do repairs, and everyone in my family treated him with the same respect as a guest. That was just the way it was. Position, rank, and status were understood; however, everyone who entered our home was treated civilly and respectfully. The lesson we learned was that everyone deserves to be treated in the way we would like to be treated.

The very skills that I learned as a child worked back then, and they work today. The same rules apply in the workplace, which functions as a type of neighborhood. Here, we need to treat each other in the way we wish to be treated. Like the neighbors we are, we must take care of each other, because at some level we know how important the office community is.

If we are going to succeed in life, we must learn and practice good manners and appropriate, proper etiquette in order to be compassionate, civil, and consistent. It's a fairly simple mission and an investment that brings tremendous returns.

A CLASS ACT LIVES BY THE RULES
OF ETIQUETTE IN BUSINESS

Here's where etiquette comes in. When I teach kids, they always ask me to explain the difference between manners and etiquette. I tell them that manners come from the inside. They are all about respecting other people and ourselves and treating them with dignity. Etiquette, on the other hand, comes from the outside. Etiquette is a set of rules that makes life orderly. Those rules change all the time, and they are different from place to place. One set is no better or worse than another set.

For example, in the United States, we shake hands when we meet someone for the first time. In Japan, people bow to one another. Shaking hands is no better or worse than bowing. What's important is knowing what to do and when to do it. When you know that, you can relax and invest your energy and brain power in the reason you happen to be there.

Rules free us. Think about how dangerous life would be if there were no traffic lights or one-way streets. If Tiger Woods wore a ski suit to play golf, what would happen to his swing? Could he still win? Could he even play the game?

This is why etiquette matters—especially in business.

So here are some etiquette rules to keep in mind at work.

1. Business etiquette is gender neutral.
2. Business etiquette is based on rank, the pecking order, hierarchy. We defer to others based on their place in the pecking order—the person with the most authority gets the attention first. It doesn't matter whether it is a man or a woman. Business etiquette is gender neutral.
3. Whoever needs the help, gets it, regardless of gender. That means if someone is carrying a box of files, we open a door for him or her to pass. Men do pull out chairs for women and open doors for them. Women must be secure enough and gracious enough to accept these kindnesses or chivalry—yet we don't have the right to expect it in the workplace.
4. Rise when someone enters your office. Come around the desk and greet them. Walk them to the door.
5. If a colleague or assistant comes into your office frequently, you don't have to rise each time. Just be sure to acknowledge them at least with eye contact and a hand gesture.

6. Address people you meet in business as Mr. or Ms. until they give you permission to use first names. Use first names only for those who give you permission or for people who are clearly your peers.

7. Never introduce yourself as Mr. or Ms. For example, "This is Mary Mitchell calling."

8. If you're the boss, it's up to you to decide how you wish subordinates to address you. Be clear about it.

9. Don't ask a subordinate to do anything for you that you would be unwilling to do yourself or for someone else.

10. Before you ask someone who works for another to do something for you, clear it first with that administrative person's boss.

11. When you introduce subordinates, say, "Michelle works with me," not "Michelle works for me."

12. Praise in public; criticize in private.

13. Never use sexist, demeaning language such as "dear," "sweetie," and "darlin'" when addressing a colleague.

14. If you go to someone else's office, wait until you are told where to sit before you take a seat.

15. Be on time for appointments.

16. Put your briefcase or bag or other paraphernalia on the floor, where it belongs, when in someone else's office. Respect their space and privacy—don't look at what's on their desk or computer screen.

17. Thank people with a handwritten note within two days of a meeting or lunch.

18. Learn elevator etiquette. If you're nearest the elevator door, enter first. If you're near the door inside the elevator, step out and let others off. Remember, the security cameras in elevators are always on, so watch what you do even when you're alone.

19. Respect others' personal space. Stand about an arm's length away. If someone backs away when you're talking, either your voice is too loud or you are crowding.

20. When you seat someone across from your desk, you send a clear message of formality and distance. Asking the person to sit either on the side of your desk or chair-to-chair without barriers sends a more harmonious message.

21. The fewer gestures you make, the more authoritatively others will perceive you.

22. Good posture demonstrates self-respect and respect for others. Your mother was right. Stand up straight. Never slouch.
23. Keep your jacket on when you walk around the workplace and when you visit someone's office for a meeting.
24. Never let an envelope leave your desk or office without the correct form of address.
25. Mr. and Ms. are the correct titles in business. Using them shows respect.
26. "Mrs." is a title for a married woman who goes by her husband's name. Her name is addressed on an invitation along with her husband's name, as in "Mr. and Mrs. John Doe." If, however, Mrs. Smith divorces Mr. Smith, she becomes "Mrs. Jane Doe" and is no longer "Mrs. John Doe."
27. People appreciate seeing their corporate titles written out. Remember, rank likes to be acknowledged.
28. Finally, if you are asking yourself "Why bother?" when you read this, remember—good manners create good relationships and good relationships create good business—not the other way around.

KEEPING THE BOSS HAPPY

Knowing how to treat the boss will benefit both of you as well as set the tone of the workplace. If the boss is stressed, you will be stressed. If you help the boss shine with his or her boss by improving productivity, boosting profits, or landing a client, your stock will soar and your days will be a whole lot more pleasant.

How to Treat The Boss

Never, ever correct or criticize your boss in public. No matter the problem, bite your tongue until you can discuss it one on one, with the door closed.

Always make your boss the first stop for any significant idea you're hatching. Bosses hate surprises. This will spare her being caught flat-footed by someone else who may ask about the project. And there may be important considerations to your great idea to which you are not privy.

ASKING FOR A RAISE

If you are good at your job, you normally acquire additional duties without receiving a commensurate increase in salary. You love what you do but you just don't feel you are earning what you deserve.

As you've probably guessed, you need to do some homework to find out what you're worth in your market. The U.S. Department of Commerce has salary figures, or you might know people in other companies who could give you some comparisons.

Second, you'll need to document both your workload and your accomplishments. Be specific. How many accounts are you tracking now, as opposed to when you started? How do you contribute to the company's success? Have you saved money through your meticulous accounting and bookkeeping, or streamlined a thorny procedure?

Once you have your facts and figures straight, rehearse the presentation you'll make to your boss. Tape it, then listen to how you sound. You want to be professional, factual, and confident. One hint of whining and you've blown it. Next, make an appointment with your boss. When you have his undivided attention, you'll be ready to make your best case.

REFOCUS YOUR PRIORITIES

Sometimes, life lands us in jobs we don't love. Or perhaps a comfortable job has grown stale. If you're someone who measures yourself by your career, these can be tough situations. It's no crime to feel out of step with your nine-to-five gig. But it's best to fix that fit as soon as possible. A tweak or two in your priorities can make your position better than ever.

First, know thyself. Be honest about your priorities. Some people live to work, but most work to live. Plan your life accordingly, without apology—even if your job is not at the top of your list.

As one Washington hotel executive puts it: "Basically, I like my job, but I resent the commitment of time required to satisfy its demands. In the meantime, we give lip service to the importance of being good parents and having solid family lives."

If that sounds like you, refocus on life off the job. That means having friends unrelated to work, activities that aren't "networking opportunities," and pleasures that don't "build skills."

Allow work to be one slice of the pie of life—and enjoy the whole thing.

Freshen your outlook. Maybe your work-life balance is fine, but your job motivation has simply stalled. If so, ask yourself why.

Perhaps you've outgrown your responsibilities. Reimagine your job in a way that would reawaken interest. Whatever your level, there may be new procedures you can develop or new duties you can assume.

Bring your manager ideas that can jump-start your motivation while improving your organization. Your initiative will look good, and a new project may be just the tonic you need.

If you can't change your job, ask around your company to see if there's a committee or other venue you can join. This will allow you to gain experience in other facets of the company, and it's an excellent opportunity for networking.

Resolving Personal Issues

Personal issues can have a big impact on job performance when they refuse to stay obediently at home while we go to work.

If personal problems are plaguing your professional life, you must deal with them—but you don't have to go it alone. Talk with your manager and explain the situation so he or she can suggest ways you might temporarily shift your duties. Remember that simple good manners and civility will always satisfy.

A CLASS ACT REMEMBERS BUSINESS CIVILITY IN EVERY BUSINESS EVENT.

CHAPTER 22

A Class Act Knows How
to Conduct Meetings with Skill

"Meetings are a great trap. Soon you find yourself trying to get agreement, and then the people who disagree come to think they have a right to be persuaded . . . However, they are indispensable when you don't want to do anything."

—John Kenneth Galbraith

OPEN YOUR MIND

Change seldom happens without challenge. Especially when we try to change our thinking. One of my favorite teachers used to say, "Be open-brained about this, okay?" Now I'm asking you to be open-brained about meetings.

Meetings have a bad reputation. Mostly everybody complains about them. I've even seen full-page ads in *The New York Times* promising that we'd never have to be bored in a meeting again if only we'd buy this little gizmo so we can do our holiday shopping, check our portfolios, make vacation plans, and check our e-mail—all the while we are held captive at a boring meeting. Talk about rude multi-tasking!

The point is, nobody talks about good meetings; only the bad ones. It's sort of like good judgment—you only notice it when it's absent.

I think that if ever there was an opportunity for individuals to shine, it is at meetings. And if we, as individuals, are dedicated to mining our own talents to contribute to a greater good, a meeting is the place to do it. Meetings are the proscenium stages for business players. Meetings are an education about every person who participates in them.

ROUND UP THE USUAL SUSPECTS

Consider the inevitable cast of characters (in the interest of efficiency, clarity, and brevity, I am using masculine examples; each character listed definitely has a female counterpart!). I've learned to identify these characters privately and thus to give myself a private laugh. That private humor takes the teeth out of their performances, thus helping me stay centered, because I don't take their behavior personally.

THE LOUNGE LIZARD sprawls all over the place, wrapping himself around chair arms and legs, sinking into any cushion in sight. Once he's in the seat, he stays there, never bothering to get up and greet others. No one would be surprised if he took off his jacket, rolled up his sleeves, and put his feet up on the coffee table. Rude, rude, rude, with an attitude of entitlement.

THE WISE GUY takes no prisoners when telling you how absurd your ideas are—no sane company would or could embrace them. He knows this because he got his "OTJ" education from Life—i.e., he has street smarts—and heaven help anyone who fails to revere them as one would a Nobel Prize. We are talking slick bully here. He thinks he's tough.

THE BOBBLE-HEAD says nary a word, offers nary a contribution. Yet every time a good idea is being put forth, the Bobble-Head nods knowingly as though he thought of it eons ago.

THE PUNDIT jumps at every chance to tell you how it was done ninety-seven years ago, or that he had come up with every new, worthy idea himself. You don't need to say anything because he already knows what you're going to say. Or so he believes. He makes homicide—his—seem like something warm and fuzzy.

This merry band of mischief-makers is familiar to us all. Why? Because it's easy to descend into any one of the personas—or all of them. And that can—and does—make a mess of any meeting. These characters make for miserable meetings. Small wonder most people consider meetings a waste of time. And what could be more disrespectful than wasting anyone's time?

THE FIVE P's

These characters have ignored the old military saw, "Remember the Five P's: Prior Planning Prevents Poor Performance." Or, as F. Lee Bailey says, "A case is won or lost before you enter the courtroom."

Meetings are places where each of us is responsible for letting our lights shine. Each of us is 100% responsible for our own communication. Each meeting-goer is responsible for helping to get to the heart of whatever matter is on the table. We accomplish this by asking, respectfully, laser-like questions. For example, what do we need to do to make that happen? Everyone in attendance is responsible for allowing his or her ideas to be challenged. We need to be willing to admit when we are wrong and also to hold fast when we are convinced we are right. In both cases, reasons must be based on facts and experience; reasons must be articulated with dignity, directness, authority, and respect. No shouting or losing one's temper.

Thus, instead of saying, "I think we should . . . " ask, "What if . . . ?"

Instead of saying, "I have a great idea . . . " ask, "Would it make sense if we . . . ?"

Instead of saying, "I want . . ." ask, "What would you think if . . . ?"

Whether we are chairing the meeting or are a participant, it's up to us to prepare, prepare, prepare.

LEARN FROM THE BEST

My mentor, Letitia Baldrige, former White House social secretary, chairs superb meetings. She learned by sitting across from heads of state. Here is Letitia's recipe for making meetings meaningful, productive, efficient, and enjoyable:

- Choose a convenient time for the meeting and provide necessary information. For example: 8 A.M. - 9 A.M. Continental breakfast will be served.

- Invite the key people who will be involved or affected by the meeting's outcome. No cast of thousands; yet no omissions.

- Distribute the agenda either by e-mail or written memo to everyone within a week of the meeting.

- Attach whatever supporting materials are required to participate fully in any discussion.

- Ensure that the meeting room is clean, neat, well-ventilated, and can accommodate all the participants comfortably.

- Always arrive early to greet the participants, shake hands, and direct them either to the conference table or to the coffee buffet. Let them know that there are place cards (double-sided) on the table.

- Supply all the attendees with a notepad, pen, and water, and make sure any audiovisual needs are met.

- Always look good; dress authoritatively and colorfully, with perfect grooming. Keep in mind that you are seen sitting, from the waist up.

- Never "over-prop" with all manner of handouts and audiovisuals that can deflect the focus from the goal.

- Begin the meeting on time, introduce everyone or ask each person to introduce himself, then briefly state the purpose and goal of the meeting and its time frame.

- Be positive and upbeat, even when challenged.

- Make it a point to recognize others' ideas, contributions, and concerns.

- Do not name-drop.

- Establish a date for the next meeting; summarize the tasks that each person attending must complete and the deadline; clearly indicate where to direct copies of any memos or reports resulting from the meeting.

- Thank everyone for taking the time to attend and participate.

WHEN ATTENDING MEETINGS, REMEMBER TO

1. **Be punctual.** You have no right to disrespect anyone's time.
2. **Look your best.** No matter how informal, no meeting is to be treated casually. When you look like a player, you will feel and behave like a player and, most importantly, be perceived as a player.
3. **Be prepared.** It's important to familiarize yourself with the meeting agenda and do whatever homework is needed. Don't subject yourself to public humiliation by being unprepared.
4. **Don't seat yourself.** The chair is responsible for that, so look for place cards or ask the chairperson where you should sit.
5. **Pay attention.** It's rude to ask anyone to repeat themselves because you were daydreaming.
6. **Zip your lip.** Never interrupt. Raise your hand to be recognized when you have something to contribute.
7. **Mind the agenda.** Don't chase rabbits and don't lead the group off into digressions that might suit your purposes yet don't serve the meeting's goal.
8. **Jettison the jokes.** Wit is one thing; relentless, wisecracking interruptions are rude, especially if they are off-color, sarcastic, or make fun of anyone.
9. **Get your signals straight.** Don't leave the meeting without clearly understanding the next steps and time frames, especially those directly impacting you. When in doubt, ask the chairperson after the meeting. It's his or her job to be sure you understand.

10. **Be a grownup.** That means don't even think about applying makeup, combing hair, clipping your nails, using your cell phone, cracking your knuckles, tapping your fingers or toes. And don't even think about showing up if you have a bad cold.
11. **Shake hands and thank the chairperson.** Someday you will be chairing a meeting and you'll appreciate being appreciated.

WHETHER CHAIRING OR ATTENDING A MEETING, ALWAYS . . .

Rehearse your key points. Don't just read the agenda. Think about it. Decide the best, most effective way to communicate your points (refer to communications section and personality styles).

Write your points or key words on index cards. I usually record myself and then play the tape back when I'm driving or unloading the dishwasher. That replicates the ambient distractions and I can tell how clearly I am coming across.

When you are introducing a new idea, the key is to make sure to go slowly. New ideas are not easy to introduce. It's a good idea to try your idea out on a trusted colleague and listen to feedback before going out on a limb for the group. We can get too close to an idea and thus ignore the big picture. And don't present new ideas as finished products. Allow others to nurture them along so they feel they've made a contribution.

Never trash the competition or decimate someone's character.

Invest in a copy of *Robert's Rules of Order* (or visit the Parliamentary Procedure Online site, http://www.parlipro.org/). It is the universally accepted meeting protocol guide. It sets forth how matters are to be presented, in what order, and how to handle dissention.

Never forget this: The people who make it look easy are usually the ones who have spent the most time in preparation.

A CLASS ACT DISPLAYS CIVILITY AT ALL MEETING EVENTS.

CHAPTER 23

A Class Act Doesn't Mix Romance with Work

"I have never yet seen anyone whose desire to build up his moral power was as strong as sexual desire."

—Confucius

As work intertwines more and more with our social lives, the relationship waters we need to navigate can easily become muddied. This means that we need to learn a whole new layer of civility to protect ourselves from inappropriate entanglements—either real or perceived. The less of your personal life you bring to work, the less chance it has to negatively affect your career. If you are dating someone from the office, courtesy is synonymous with discretion.

A CORPORATE POLICY ON DATING

If you're lucky, your company has a dating policy that is designed to protect everyone against discomfort and legal liability. It's a good idea to familiarize yourself with such a policy if it exists at your place of business before any specific need arises. This is most important because you must be aware of dating policies before you enter into a relationship, since some policies require disclosure, especially when unequal ranks are concerned. Others require one partner to transfer departments or require both partners to sign a contract of consent, basically agreeing not to bring suit against the company or each other if the relationship sours.

If your company has no articulated formal policy, take an objective look at the corporate culture. The only way to survive, much less thrive, in any company is to learn to function within the organization according to its rules, and many of them are unwritten.

DON'T FLAUNT YOUR RELATIONSHIP

The number one rule concerning a workplace romance is *don't advertise it*, no matter what your corporate culture seems to accept. You can be sure that co-workers and top brass alike will be a whole lot more tolerant of your relationship if they are not made to feel awkward over it.

Not advertising your relationship means that not only should you refrain from discussing your relationship with anyone in the office, your guard should go up if someone asks you about it—especially if it is new and unproved. If you are caught in this situation, a good answer might sound like, "Why would you ask me that?" The best defense often is a good offense. Your unassailably professional behavior will defend you against office gossip. Good seldom results from office gossip. Others may resent your happiness and judge your job performance in light of your "distractions." Besides, if the romance ends while still in its formative stage, you'll be mighty glad you never discussed it with anyone.

Consider this ethical consideration as well: flaunting your office romance

invites conversation about your private life. Conversation and concern about one's private life when you're "on the clock" infringes on both time and energy owed the company and is a way of devaluing an employee's contribution. If you cause yourself to be a topic of conversation and thereby cause others within the company to focus on something other than the company's work, then you are cheating the company. Cheating is unethical, not to mention bad manners.

THINK BEFORE YOU ASK A CO-WORKER OR CLIENT FOR A DATE

At the beginning of any romance, wisdom and prudence caution us against rushing in. All the more so in office romances. Be careful that the client or customer you invite for a date won't think you're being overly aggressive. Adopt an awkward teenage mode and get some sense of whether your dating attentions will be welcome.

Before you ask for a date, stop and think—do you have a friendly professional rapport already? Nobody should be hit broadside with an invitation for a date. Do eye contact and smiles come easily when you speak to each other? If so, that could be an auspicious beginning. Go ahead. Invite the person for a date. Make it for something fun and non-threatening, such as a sports event or Sunday brunch at a friend's. Daylight fosters ease and comfort. Keep the date innocent.

Should you get turned down, you'll need to rely on your gut to tell you whether to ask again. People do make plans, and it's not impossible that your invitee had some that conflicted with your invitation. Remember two things: one, the workplace is not a singles bar; and two, don't confuse dating with sales and an attempt to wear someone down with persistent persuasion. Your "friendly persuasion" might be someone else's sexual harassment. Play it cool. Perceptions are reality. We can't argue with how a person feels—if someone is feeling harassed, it's a disaster waiting to happen.

SUPERIORS DATING SUBORDINATES

Work life gets especially dicey when a supervisor dates a subordinate. Even when both people are completely professional, the supervisory decisions and choices will be filtered through lenses of perceived favoritism. Understandably, this creates a negative atmosphere for everyone in the department. For the couple involved, the supervisor will be viewed as playing favorites; the subordinate's professional contributions will be diminished or, worse, dismissed. Should the relationship die, the perceptions will live on. Both parties will be remembered for their affair, period. Think about it. If someone asks you, "What is the first thing that comes to mind about the Clinton presidency?" you'll probably reply, "Monica Lewinsky."

If you are in a romance with someone on a different corporate level, it is even more important to be well-versed on whatever HR policies are in place and to speak with the HR person or a higher-ranking person in the company. Don't expect that person to make decisions for you. As a couple, you should first think through your options and prioritize them. It's likely that the person of greater authority will have a useful perspective. Still, go into this type of office romance with your eyes wide open, knowing that you will emerge on a course of change. Changes may range from transferring departments to finding a new job in a new company. Like any dating situation, these are life decisions, not to be taken lightly, and must be made rationally. Additionally, not only are two individuals involved; their decisions impact their relationship, their department, and the company.

WHAT IF ALL GOES WELL . . .

Let's suppose your relationship blossoms into something wonderful that's likely to last. Your office frowns on dating among co-workers. As with any situation, you have three choices. You can accept it. You can leave the job. You can change it.

Translated into the workplace romance scenario, your choices are to continue the relationship in secret, ask for a transfer, end the relationship, or find a new job. Only you can make this decision. Once your relationship has stood the test of some time—let's say three months—it's a good idea to speak confidentially to your supervisor or HR person about your options.

No company wants to lose good people—especially when they are doing their best to play by its rules.

THE BIG PICTURE, IN BRIEF

Here are some guidelines to keep you focused on the big picture at work:

1. If you can't work with someone, forget about dating that person. Chemistry causes combustion as well as harmony. You need to feel secure about a work relationship before you take it to another level.
2. Put on the brakes and keep them on. It's true; everybody loves a lover . . . for about five minutes. Then those courting rituals—the overly frequent trips past each other's desk; the instant messaging all day long; the "I just called to say I love you" telephoning—become a sophomoric intrusion on the workplace.
3. Recognize and accept a dual relationship. Be mature about it. That old saw, "You marry the person and his or her family" is especially true here. In other words, there is a lot of baggage in office romances. Both parties will need to be able to communicate with each other and to see matters from the others' point of view. Both parties will need to accept the fact that they are subjecting themselves to a higher professional standard, if for no other reason than to overcome the distractions of being in love with love. And how will you handle it if you break up and still need to work side by side?

WHAT NOT TO DO

Here is a list of Don'ts to help you steer clear of romantic disasters at work:

1. Don't stay at office parties later than 6 P.M. Remember: perceptions are reality. Lingering at a party's end signals that you are inviting continued partying. If you leave, late, with someone, tongues will wag about how you spent the rest of the evening—even if you just walked to the bus stop together and went your separate ways. Never forget that when it comes to office parties, the emphasis belongs on the "office," not on the "party."

2. Don't talk about your troubles with your spouse or lover. You can't count on others keeping your secrets. Remember that childhood game, "Whisper Down the Lane"? Remember, too, that people switch alliances more often than we think. Your current lover might end up your confidante's next conquest. The less everybody knows about personal matters, the better. If you're troubled about a relationship, invest in a professional counselor.

3. Don't tell off-color stories. Others might see naughty tales as a come-on. They are embarrassing to everyone. Besides, although few have the guts to express their discomfort and disapproval of your storytelling, you run the risk of being excluded from important projects, groups, meetings, and social events for reasons you might never be told about it.

4. Don't talk about your body—especially anything you feel needs expansion or reduction. That's like telling someone not to think about the color blue. Can you see any other color? At that point, blue becomes the only color. Thus, you might be talking about the surgical safety of breast augmentation or reduction—and you can be sure that all the other person can see and think about is your chest. That can sound like a come-on; at the very least it can create a sexually uncomfortable atmosphere.

5. Don't go bar hopping with co-workers of the opposite sex, or potential dates. You're just asking for morning-after gossip—that you don't need. And alcohol stimulates loose lips. We all know that loose lips sink ships.

6. Don't ever discuss a sexual experience with anyone in the office—male or female. It's stupid. It's bad manners because such confessions seldom are comfortable conversations—yet the confidante seldom has the guts to say, "That's really a whole lot more than I need or want to hear." It's also bad strategy. Remember office gossip.

7. Don't ever say to a co-worker, "If I weren't (read: married, involved with someone, etc.), I could get into a lot of trouble with you." Sounds corny, but variations on this theme are alive and well. Although it might be said without guile, you don't want to learn later that you made a pass at someone.

8. Don't indulge in PDAs (public displays of affection). That goes for long conversations during work; lunch taken for too long and at irregular hours for what might seem irregular purposes; and walking in to work together in the morning, bleary-eyed. If you are dating someone in the office, it is very smart to be cool and not be seen kissing, hugging, or casting sug-

gestive glances at one another. The sight of two people demonstrating physical attraction in the office stops people in their tracks, no matter how charming they may find it. It distracts and stops work from progressing as it should.

Certainly there have been office romances that have gone undiscovered— but, so far as I know, only in the minds of the principals. Even when nothing is happening, there is office talk. And office talk is something to be reckoned with. So keep cause for talk to a minimum. At the very least, remain mum during those few casual dates. It's your private life, and you should keep it private. Your relationship may not last. If it doesn't, you'll still have to work with someone who once was your lover. You'll have to be civilized about it.

AND IF YOU DO GET CAUGHT RED-FACED . . .

So, what do you do if your "secret" office romance gets the better of you and that rule against anything more than a friendly hello is broken? You are in the conference room, sharing an innocent embrace and kiss, when an unsuspecting colleague walks in on you.

Instead of getting flustered and red-faced and stammering out an explanation, try to be mature about it. Look the person in eye, take an even breath, and try to calm down. Acknowledge that the situation is embarrassing for all of you and say something like, "I would appreciate that you never saw this."

All of the above assumes that you were not caught with someone else's spouse or significant other. It also assumes that you weren't violating any personal commitments to another person. If you were, then you need a lot more than etiquette advice to clean this up.

A CLASS ACT PROJECTS AND PRCTICES CIVILITY IN ALL OFFICE RELATIONSHIPS.

CHAPTER 24

When a Class Act Works Successfully from Home

"Nothing is really work unless you would rather be doing something else."

—James Matthew Barrie

THE UPS AND DOWNS OF WORKING FROM HOME

Initially, understand that the rules that apply are different for the corporate employee working at home and for the self-employed working at home. When I began my business in Philadelphia, I had a posh address and a staff of seven. Not that I really could afford the overhead, but outside perceptions demanded such accoutrements. Without them, you had no substance, no staying power, and thus no magnetism for important assignments.

Things are different today. Major companies such as Merck, Lexis-Nexis, and KPMG are advocating and supporting home offices for their key employees and managers. Consumers have demonstrated that one's ability to provide a service does not depend on bricks and mortar.

Personal Issues

Your Image Remains the Key. Perceptions are important. Professional is as professional does. While home-based workers needn't don business suits every day, they simply won't feel as professional or be perceived that way doing business in slippers and flannel pajamas, unshowered and unshaven. We need to put on street clothes, even if alone, because how we dress directly affects our job performance. If we dress for work, we can consider ourselves at work and thereby deal with the distractions and interpersonal relationships that are inherent to this type of work environment.

Familial Concerns

First, there's your family. Although I have been consulting and training for a decade, have written a syndicated newspaper column for as long, and have published four books with two more appearing soon, my siblings still don't believe I work.

More specifically, they refuse to accept the fact that I have a real job. Here's how that looks in daily life: I am at home and thus am accessible and available at all times. I've learned the hard way that getting defensive and emotional only fuels the perception of the silly little dilettante doing a bit of something creative to feel validated. Instead, I took a few positive and concrete steps. First, I eliminated the home telephone line from my office. Next, I told the family that if they wanted to reach me during work hours, the work line was their best bet.

It's important to provide this information in a voice as unemotional as though you were saying, "It's raining outside."

Setting 'Office' Hours

As for work hours, even though I am self-employed, I'd like to tell you that I established a real schedule. The truth is that I often can be found before dawn and after dark at my computer, should the opportunity and the motivation prevail. However, I turn off the telephone ringer at 6 P.M. and back on again at 9 A.M. During that time, a reliable voicemail service picks up messages. In short, I trained my family and myself. You must realize that if you are a company employee, there will be parameters on hours and availability which need be met.

Resolving Conflicts

Part of that training process includes Conflict Resolution 101. In short, as unemotionally (sounding) as possible, acknowledge their momentary piques and objections and then state the reality of your situation.

That sounds like, "I know you want me to take you to the mall, sweetie, and you know that this is the middle of my workday. Let's work out a good time for us both, okay?"

Again, the key to success is the "it's raining outside" tone of voice. The very minute anybody gets you on the defensive, you'll be into apologies and breaking your own rules. Nobody will win—not you, not your family, and certainly not your clients and especially not your employer, if that's the case.

Houseguests, too, deserve to be told your work arrangements. Do this well in advance, so they don't assume a Tuesday while the kids are at school means you are as free as a bird to play. That is, unless you schedule that free time.

Hiring Child Care

Feeling like a competent professional is often easier in a skyscraper. When you're at home, your behavior dictates how you end up feeling about your-self—not the other way around.

It's a good idea to hire some childcare help, even while you are at home (an employer might well require such an arrangement). It's worth the invest-ment in professional effectiveness as well as family harmony. Having some-one to take care of your kids, thereby making contact with you off limits during the workday, will help your offspring perceive you as a working pro-fessional.

A Sound Body Leads to a Sound Mind

Finally, take good care of yourself. For one thing, you'll need to exercise more to compensate for your decreased mobility. Getting oxygen to the brain and other important parts factors significantly in effective relationships—it helps one play with a full deck, so to speak.

For another, how you feel about yourself will contribute significantly to being flexible and thus able to serve your clients and family well. Don't expect to perform well if you are stressed out and feeling deprived.

Sometimes it takes more discipline to schedule being good to ourselves than to work harder and longer. Perhaps it is possible to pay someone to do the latter; only we can accomplish the former.

Positioning Your Business for Success

Since you are the operating business professional, you know what is expected if you are an employee as well as what you need to do as an entrepreneur. That governs the kind of external communications decisions you make. For example, my own business serves fairly high-end and luxury clients, especially those in service industries. Thus, my stationery is the finest quality paper and it's engraved with the company name, address, and contact information. It makes sense. If, however, I were a social worker working from home, that same stationery would appear pretentious. It wouldn't make sense.

Thoughtfully and accurately, present your residential office operation for maximum impact. Don't pretend that your business is greater than it really is. Otherwise, you set up unrealistic expectations and worse, appear grandiose—never a plus in good business relationships. For instance, if you operate sans secretary, don't add phony initials to the bottom of your letters to make it seem as though your secretary has processed the document.

As an entrepreneur, your business name, logo, stationery, and your marketing efforts all send important messages about you and your work. Think those decisions through. Sometimes our "best" creative efforts end up being white elephants. My own first business stationery, I learned expensively, looked great in the hand but photocopied miserably.

Looking back, I have to admit that I spent more energy making decisions about how to cut my hair than I did strategically considering the implications of my communications. That proved expensive and, at times, embarrassing. Consider what you call your business. Is it too trendy? Does it project the image that aligns with your market? Does it sound stable and professional? How does it sound when spoken? Is it difficult to say or spell when giving or receiving messages? Is it too close for comfort to any other business names? You may go through the exercise of posing all these questions only to decide that your own name works best. That's how I ended up—and I'm glad I did.

Your e-mail name bears the same kind of close scrutiny. Simple is better; straightforward is better.

Language drives design. When it comes to your business name, the words drive the design. Too many of us opt for a fancy design that ends up being outdated too soon, requiring costly updates and re-dos. Err on the side of caution here. Search out attractive, readable typefaces, ink, and paper colors. Think in terms of their end use—stationery, memos, e-zines, advertising. Make sure they reproduce easily and clearly. Invest in a reputable graphic designer. You'll find, though, that doing your homework will substantially contain those costs. In other words, only take your concept to a designer once you are clear about it. Before that time, when you're in the infancy of your home-based business, opt for simple one-color printing on a quality stock.

Don't overbuy. Until you are established, buy in limited quantities that allow you to refine and change your mind or direction without ending up with too much surplus. Work on the trial-and-error model. The key here is that whatever you do, do it professionally.

THE BRANCH OFFICE—YOUR CAR

If you lovingly call your home office your worldwide headquarters, then your car becomes your branch office. I remember a home-office worker apologizing for her messy car and saying, "it's a reflection of my state of mind." Scary thought. She said it in jest; but it sent up a red flag. Remember that what's on the inside is projected on the outside.

Whether a telecommuter for a major corporation operating at least in part from your home, or an entrepreneur whose business office is located in your residence, remember you must always behave like a CLASS ACT. Whether in your "office," at home, or in a car, the setting always must be appropriate for professional conduct and accomplishment.

It's more likely your clients will see your car before they see your office space, during those countless runs to the post office, clients' offices, and the like. That's why it's essential that your vehicle projects the message that you are a Class Act. Just as you don't necessarily need a new Armani suit to make a positive impression, you don't necessarily need a new Lexus or Mercedes-Benz. But just as you do need to be perfectly groomed in business, your car needs to be neat and well maintained.

Make sure you pay attention to the maintenance requirements for oil changes and service. You don't want to break down en route to an important meeting. Keep it clean—trash those Starbucks cups and protein-bar wrappers. If you don't own a car vacuum, invest some elbow grease and quarters in a drive-through car wash vacuum station. Don't be a magnet for junk. That goes for the trunk, too.

ESTABLISH RITUALS

Recognizing that office and professional discipline in the home workspace will need to be self-imposed, work out a time schedule for a walk around the block morning and afternoon, regular times for post office or supply runs, and rigorous hours. For the flexible work arrangement to succeed, constant evaluation and attention is necessary. Be sure your co-workers at the business's office as well as your client knows the home-office arrangement.

A CLASS ACT RECOGNIZES THAT WHEN THE OUTER APPEARANCE OF OUR WORK IS AS SOLID AS OUR MOST ACCOMPLISHED RESULTS, WE FEEL BETTER. WHEN WE FEEL BETTER, WE BECOME MORE CONFIDENT. AND THE MORE CONFIDENT WE ARE, THE BETTER WORK WE DO.

Part VI

FOOD AND DRINK

CHAPTER 25

A Class Act at Table

"The world was my oyster, until I used the wrong fork."
—Oscar Wilde

THE ETIQUETTE OF DINING

There is a very real unspoken prejudice against people who don't know how to handle themselves skillfully at table. Unfortunately, no one ever will tell you that they prefer not to do business with you because you eat like a pig. The following are the key points that will help you to make the best impression.

Cutlery

Don't hold your fork like a cello or your knife like Lady Macbeth's dagger. In addition, don't wave your cutlery triumphantly in the air to emphasize a point, and never place silverware partly on the table and partly on the plate.

After you pick up a piece of cutlery, it should never touch the table again. Knives go fully on the plate, blade facing in. No resting tips on the plate and handles on the table like a gangplank. And yes, your mother was right. Work from the outside in if you're not sure what utensil to use.

Napkins

Gently unfold the napkin and place it on your lap.

Dab your mouth delicately with the napkin to remove traces of food or drink. Don't blot or rub the lower half of your face.

Don't flap or wave it around like a flag. If you leave the table, place your napkin on the chair seat and push the chair back under the table. Gently. Watch the upholstery.

At the end of the meal, place your napkin loosely on the table to the left of your plate. Don't refold your napkin at the end of the meal, because an unknowing server might give it to another diner.

Chewing

No matter how urgently you want to inject the perfect kernel of wit and wisdom at just the right moment, never speak with food in your mouth.

Finish chewing, swallow, and smile philosophically, content in the knowledge that you could have said just the right thing but were too refined to speak with food in your mouth. Don't gulp and blurt.

Never chew with your mouth open.

Appearance

Remember what your mother said: Sit up straight and keep your elbows off the table. If you have any doubt about where your hands belong, keep them in your lap.

Breaking Bread

Tear bread into bite-size pieces and butter each piece just before you eat it. Don't butter the entire slice of bread or the entire roll to get it ready for occasional bites during the course of the meal.

Speed

Take it easy. Whether you're at The Ritz or Gertie's Grease Pit, gulping down food is not only unhealthy but also unattractive, and it can cross the line into rudeness when dining with others.

Dining partners should have the same number of courses and start and finish each one at about the same time. Don't be dawdling over your soup while others are waiting for dessert or vice versa.

Don't Pick Your Teeth!

If you have something trapped between your teeth, don't pick at it while you are at the table. If it's really driving you nuts, excuse yourself, go to the restroom, and pick to your heart's content.

Lipstick Etiquette

Leaving behind a trail of lipstick on stemware and flatware is bad form, especially at a business meal. If you apply lipstick in the restaurant (which I personally find pretty tacky) and don't have a blotting tissue with you, make a detour to the restroom or nab a cocktail napkin from the bar on your way to the table.

Smoking

Even if you're sitting in the smoking section of the restaurant, you should never light up between courses. It affects your dining partners' taste buds and is a jarring note during any meal.

Wait until after dessert and, even then, ask if anyone minds if you smoke. If anyone does object, offer to wait or to smoke at the bar. And please, never use a plate as an ashtray.

Handbags and Briefcases

Keep handbags and briefcases off the table. And this rule goes for keys, hats, gloves, eyeglasses, eyeglass cases, wallets, cigarette packs, and cell phones. In short, if it isn't part of the meal, it shouldn't be on the table.

Don't Panic!

Having spent so much time on mistakes, it is important to point out that nothing as diverse as dining with a number of other people ever will be achieved with perfect serenity. Things go wrong, and when they do, do your best to react calmly and, if possible, cheerfully.

FURTHER DINING-TABLE GUIDELINES THAT ALWAYS APPLY

- When you're finished eating, don't scrape and stack the plates, and don't push your plate away. Correctly placing your flatware will communicate to your server that you're finished. The "finished" position for flatware means placing fork and knife diagonally parallel across the plate. Imagine the face of a clock on which the tips of your knife and fork, fork inside knife, are positioned at 10:20.

- Never crumble crackers into soup.

- Don't blow on any liquid or food that's too hot to eat. Wait until it cools and eat from the sides of the bowl first.

- Don't dunk—not even doughnuts at breakfast. It's fine to break one piece of bread at a time and pick it up with your fork to soak up sauce or gravy.

- Fish bones are removed with your thumb and index finger and then put on the edge of the plate.

- Hold red wine and brandy by the bowl of the glass, because your hand's warmth helps release its bouquet.

- Hold glasses of white wine and champagne by the stem to keep the temperature cool. It's fine to hold both red and white wine glasses by the stem should you get confused.

- When packets of sweetener or sugar are served with tea or coffee, tuck the empty paper under the edge of the saucer or place it in the ashtray if no one is going to be smoking.

- When you pass food around the table, pass to your right.

- Pass the rolls, butter, condiments, cream, and sugar when that part of the meal is being eaten, even if you're not having any. Pass the salt and pepper shaker together. Place the cream and sugar on the table within reach of the person who needs them.

- Pass gravy boats, pitchers, and creamers with the handle facing the next person.

- If you want something that's not within reach, ask someone to pass it to you.

A CLASS ACT'S DEMEANOR AT TABLE

Since dining is not an "every person for himself/herself" experience, especially in the business arena, your general demeanor at the table is important. Here are some tips:

- Remember to convey your food to your mouth, not the other way around.

- Don't ask people where they're going when they leave the table and don't leap to volunteer directions without being asked.

- If you need to use the facilities, excuse yourself and leave quietly.

- Take medicine discreetly, preferably away from the table. If you do take medicine at the table, don't comment about it. No explanation is necessary, and complaints or descriptions are seldom welcome.

- If you belch, cover your mouth with your napkin and quietly say, "Excuse me" to nobody in particular.

- You don't have to thank your server repeatedly. Let the service be unobtrusive as possible; and if you are served something while you are talking, don't stop.

- Don't affect pretensions of perfect French, Italian, or any language, wine knowledge, or food expertise unless it's genuine. That's a quick way to look like a fool.

- Accidents happen to everyone. React in as low-key fashion as possible. If you spill or break something, unobtrusively bring it to your server's attention. Blot up what you can and let the mishap's victim take care of himself.

- If there's a problem with service, the host should excuse himself from the table and speak quietly with the manager to request a different server. Guests should never complain about service. If, inadvertently, you are served food that has gone off, quietly tell your host, who should deal with the server and request a replacement.

- When declining alcohol, simply say something like, "I don't think I'll have any wine today." That way, by your statement and using the word "today," you remove any judgment about the consumption of alcohol, both as host and guest.

HOW A CLASS ACT HANDLES TRICKY FOODS

Artichokes are eaten with the fingers, removing one leaf at a time. Dip the soft end into the sauce and pull it through your teeth to remove the edible part. Discard the rest. Use a knife to scrape the fuzzy part off the heart and then eat it with a fork and knife, dipping it first into the sauce offered.

Asparagus is considered finger food in Europe. In the United States it can be eaten as finger food, provided there's no drippy sauce, or by cutting each stem into inch-sized pieces and eating them with a fork.

Avocados are eaten either with a spoon from their shells or with a fork when cut into pieces.

Bacon should be eaten with a fork and knife unless it's very crisp; then you can eat it with your fingers.

Bananas are eaten with a knife and fork after peeling when served at the table. If not at table, peel and eat as you go.

Berries should be eaten with a spoon, except for strawberries served with stems, which are held by the stem and eaten in a bite or two after dipping into sugar or sauce.

Cake can be eaten with fingers if it's cut bite-sized and not sticky. Use a fork if not; if served with sauce or ice cream, use both fork and spoon. Hold the spoon in your right hand, using the fork as a pusher in your left.

Caviar should be spread on toast with a knife and eaten with your fingers.

Celery, Olives, Pickles, and Radishes should be taken from the serving piece with your fingers and placed on the side of your dinner plate. Eat them with your fingers. If olives are large and unpitted, hold one in your fingers and eat it with several small bites. If pitted, eat them whole.

Chicken and Fowl require knife and fork unless served at a picnic, when it's fine to eat with your fingers.

Corn on the Cob should be eaten with two hands while holding the ear. Butter a few rows at a time only and eat them before going on for more. This is a food only served at very casual occasions and not in Europe, where it is considered food for livestock. On picnics, count on three large paper napkins per person!

Eggs. Use your fork for hard-boiled eggs. Use a spoon to eat soft-boiled eggs directly from the shell. Use your knife to slice off the cap. You can also scoop soft-boiled eggs from the shell into a small plate and eat them with a spoon.

Grapefruit halves should be sectioned so the meat is easily obtained. Eat the sections with a spoon and never squeeze the juice.

Lemon wedges are secured by the fork and pressed with the other hand. It is also acceptable to pick them up with your fingers and press the juice out. "Lemon panties" are cheesecloth sleeves with an elastic band, designed to fit over a lemon cut in half, so as one squeezes the lemon, it contains the seeds. These usually are used in upscale restaurants that serve lobster and seafood.

Lobsters should be eaten with a seafood fork to extract the meat after the claws have been cracked with a nutcracker. Cut large pieces first with a fork. Pull off the small claws and clean them as if you were drawing through a straw, eat stuffed lobster with a knife and fork. Hard-shelled crabs are eaten just like lobster.

Oranges and Tangerines should be peeled with a sharp knife or the fingers and then eaten section by section with the fingers. If served on a plate in slices, use your fork.

Peaches should be halved, then quartered with a knife, and eaten with a fork. It's fine to eat the skin or to pull it away from the flesh with a knife or your fingers.

Pineapple is eaten with either a spoon, when served in small pieces, or a fork, when sliced.

Potatoes. Eat baked potatoes from the skin with a fork, then eat the skin with knife and fork if you like. Add butter from your butter plate with a fork, but do not mash the contents of the potato. Chips and shoestring potatoes are finger food. French fries should be cut in half and eaten with a fork.

Sandwiches. Use a knife and fork to eat open-faced sandwiches. Large sandwiches should be cut into quarters to eat with the fingers or use a knife and fork. Tea sandwiches and canapés are finger food.

Shrimp are eaten with fingers if tails are left on. Shrimp cocktail is eaten with a seafood fork in two bites if large. Better still to place them on a serving plate and cut with knife and fork. Don't try to eat the tabs left on shrimp at a cocktail party. Discard them in any little plate you find, or crumble them in a cocktail napkin.

Spaghetti is eaten a few strands at a time, twirling them around the tines of your fork, Some persons support the spaghetti with a spoon, but this is not considered refined, especially in Europe. Small-sized pasta, such as ziti, penne, etc., require only a fork. You can use a piece of a roll as a "pusher" if you're having a hard time.

Tortillas are eaten from the end, rolled up on the hand or plate.

Watermelon, when cut into small pieces, is eaten with a spoon, Otherwise, use your fork. Put the seeds into the palm of your hand to transfer to the side of the plate. If you're eating it out of doors, forget cutlery, but don't ever spit the seeds.

A CLASS ACT IS A MODEL OF CIVILITY AT TABLE.

CHAPTER 26

A Class Act at the Formal Meal, Buffet, Banquet

"Sharing food with another human being is an intimate act that should not be indulged in lightly."

—M.F.K. Fisher

THE FORMAL MEAL

Don't feel alone if you panic when opening an invitation to a formal dinner. Many of us feel that way. The truth is, you are probably less likely to encounter the unknown at a formal dinner than at any other social gathering.

The more formal the dinner, the more predictable it is. And, once you know what to expect, you will know what to do and be able to relax and enjoy the event.

Arrival

After stopping at the restroom to check your general appearance and make any necessary repairs, proceed to the table. A server will draw the chair for you. Enter from your left. Remark on how grand the table looks.

As others arrive, remember that gentlemen must rise to meet newcomers.

When you are all seated, wait for the host to place the napkin in his or her lap first before placing yours in your lap unfolded.

The Place Setting

It's easy to be dazzled by the place settings of a formal dinner table. Spend some time looking at the diagram below to become familiar with all the accoutrements.

- Knives and spoons are on your right.

- Forks and napkins are on your left. The single exception is the cocktail fork, which will be farthest right, if there is a seafood course.

- Glasses are on your right. Notice the different shapes of the glasses for different wines or champagne and that the largest glass is your water goblet.

- Plates for solid foods, such as salad and bread, are to your left.

- Note the dessert spoon and fork above your plate.

- Generally, you will start using your utensils from the outside as the courses are served.

- Knives and forks are placed on the right, and forks and napkins on the left. Liquids are on the right, and solids (such as a bread plate) are on the left. Confusion comes easily when we're sitting at an overcrowded table.

- Use cutlery from the outside in. If someone commandeers your bread plate, use the side of your dinner plate.

- Here's a discreet tip: Hold your hands in front of you and make a circle with each thumb and index finger. Hold the other fingers

straight up. Your right hand will form a "d" and your left will form a "b". See? Drinks on the right; bread on the left.

THE WINE SERVICE

Wine will be served during the first course, which is the soup course.

The server will approach you from the right. If you don't want wine, place your fingertips on the rim of your wine glass and say, "I'm not having any today (or tonight)." Qualifying your refusal in this manner indicates that you do not disapprove of others enjoying wine with dinner.

White wine and champagne glasses are always held by the stem; red wine glasses may be held by the stem as well. Most often red wine is held by the goblet. The warmth of your hand releases the bouquet.

Toasting Tips

- If you are being toasted, don't put your hand on your glass or drink.

- You don't need to be drinking alcohol to toast. Water will do.

- Don't clink glasses with someone else; it's bad for the glassware.

- Toasts should be sincere, brief, and not read, but memorized.

- Toast the host in return if you are the honored guest; after the host's toast or following the meal is fine.

- Don't tap on your glass to get attention.

- The host is always the first to toast.

THE COURSES

The clue to how many courses there will be is the number of pieces of silverware, although sometimes silver is replaced between courses. Most formal dinners have seven courses that are served in this order:

1. Soup
2. Fish
3. Sorbet, to cleanse the palate
4. A meat or fowl dish
5. Salad, often served with cheese
6. Dessert
7. Coffee

If you remember the following rules about formal dinners you should have no difficulty in appearing as if you've eaten this way your entire life. Being comfortable at the meal will also allow you to enjoy the food and the company. Courses are served from the left and removed from the right. Liquids are poured and cleared from the right.

- Try to finish each course at the same time as your fellow diners. When you have finished with a course, signal the server with your flatware in the following way: Visualize a clock face on your plate. Place the knife and fork in the 10:20 position with the points at 10 and the handles at 4. The prongs of the fork may be up or down, but the knife blade should be facing you.

· To send the message that you are just taking a temporary break from eating, cross the knife and fork on your plate with the fork over the knife and the prongs pointing down. The knife blade should be at the 10 o'clock position and the fork prongs at the 2 o'clock position with the handle at 8 o'clock.

· When the first course of soup is served, tilt the spoon away from you at the outer edge of the soup plate first. To access the last of the soup, you may tilt the soup plate away from you. When you have finished, leave the soup spoon in the soup plate.

· Refreshing ices or sorbets date back as far as the Roman Empire. They are only used now to cleanse the palate after the fish course. You may eat the garnish, which may be mint leaves, herbs, or flower petals. The spoon for this course will not be part of the place setting. It will be served with the sorbet.

· Remember when cutting the meat or fowl of the next course to only cut enough for one mouthful at a time.

· The salad course comes with its own knife and fork. Use the salad knife to put cheese on crackers or bread.

· If dessert is served with both fork and spoon, use the spoon in the right hand for eating and the fork for pushing with the other hand.

· When finished stirring your coffee, put the spoon on the saucer. Do not put the spoon in your mouth.

AFTERNOON TEA AND HIGH TEA

For an informal relaxed meeting later in the day, but without alcohol, tea is a nice possibility. Afternoon tea in the United States begins in some hotels at 3:30 p.m. In England, without fail, it begins at 4 o'clock.

Tea consists of finger sandwiches first, followed by scones with jam, apple butter, or clotted cream. Cut the scones in half before adorning them. Miniature fruit tarts and pastries may be served as well.

High tea is generally served between 5:30 and 7:30 in the evening and is a hearty meal. It begins with fish or meat served with treacle. Roast chicken, ham, pork, poached salmon, whole-grain breads, Cornish pasties, and meat pies are also traditional foods for this occasion.

BRAVING THE BUFFET—DON'T BE BAFFLED

The buffet meal scene may resemble the siege of the Bastille. Somehow, ordinarily sensible people seem to think the food will be taken away before they get some or that others will take all of the food, leaving them to starve. This irrational approach results in the two major buffet blunders: approaching the table too quickly and putting too much food on your plate.

Approach

Always view the entire buffet discreetly so you can pre-determine your choices and not find yourself with a mountain on your plate halfway along. Before piling food on your plate, look at the dining tables. If utensils and/or plates are already there, you don't need to look for them at the buffet table. Remember, if place cards are on the tables, do not shift them around to suit yourself.

Then take a look to see whether the buffet has one or two lines. If two lines are moving, you will find serving utensils on both sides of the table.

Take your place at the end of the line. Gender and status privileges do not apply in the buffet line, so don't try to get ahead of anyone and don't break up a couple or a group going through the line together.

Dishing

If one item is in short supply, go easy on it. At a restaurant or hotel, it is fine to ask to have a dish replenished. At a private party, don't ask.

Use the serving spoon or fork provided for a particular dish, and put the serving piece next to the platter or chafing dish when you are finished. A hot metal spoon in a chafing dish could burn the fingers of another diner.

Don't overload your dish. Going back for seconds or thirds is perfectly acceptable. Don't take platefuls of food for the table. That defeats the whole idea of a buffet, which is offering a multitude of choices for a variety of tastes and appetites.

Serving Stations

When various dishes are served at serving stations, as at a brunch buffet, remember that the attendants are limited in what they can provide. Special requests are okay as long as they are easily accomplished.

For example, you can ask for scrambled eggs at the omelet station, but don't ask for "sunny side up" if no whole eggs are in sight. And only ask for ingredients in your omelet that are in sight and readily available. Similarly, don't ask for an end cut of beef if you don't see one.

Plates

In a restaurant, plenty of clean, freshly polished plates should be available, which means you should not have to reuse a plate. When you're going back to the buffet for seconds, don't hesitate to ask a server to replace a plate or silverware or retrieve what you need at the buffet table.

In a private home, use common sense to determine whether you should retain your plate or ask for a new one. In any case, never scrape and stack your plates when you're finished.

Eating While Sitting Down

If people invite you to join their table as you leave the buffet line, either accept graciously or find a way to decline just as graciously. For instance, you could say, "I'm sorry, but I promised Tom and his family that I'd eat with them."

Even though people at your table will be sitting down to eat at different times, it's still a good idea to generally keep pace with others at the table and engage them in conversation. If you need to leave the table temporarily, be sure to place your napkin on the seat or arm of your chair.

Eating While Standing

If you're eating while standing up, it's even more important to avoid over-loading your plate. That way you can circulate a bit.

Indeed, one of the few—maybe the only—advantages of a stand-up buffet is that you can drift around and chat with a lot of people. For example, food at cocktail parties is often consumed while standing. When you settle on a place to stand, make sure you are not blocking a path to the buffet table or anything else.

A CLASS ACT EXHIBITS CIVILITY AT THE FORMAL MEAL, BUFFET, BANQUET, AND TEA.

CHAPTER 27

A Class Act at Cocktail Parties and Receptions

"Heroes are made in battles, but losers are made in cocktail gatherings."
—Anon.

Cocktail parties are filled with opportunity, but they can be minefields. If we consider cocktail parties as opportunities, they provide us a setting to shine that's different from how our colleagues see us on the job. For example, suppose you are in the MIS division of your company, yet you long to be in sales. A social setting provides the perfect place to the meet people who would be able to support your goal and even help you get there. But aside from being the perfect opportunity to meet people, cocktail parties are also anxiety-provoking for some people. The fact is that most adults feel a lot of anxiety about walking into a roomful of strangers. Knowing this gives you the perfect opportunity to be a party hero just by being aware of, and willing to draw out, the loner in the corner; to smile at people you don't know; by being full of positive, upbeat energy. All of these actions can help your career, as you will be recognized as a helpful, competent human being in a social setting—A CLASS ACT.

REMEMBER: BUSINESS IS BUSINESS

We are invited to business social events for any or all of three reasons:

- The host wants our business

- The host wants to thank us for our business

- The host believes we have something to contribute to the party's success

A business social event is just that: business. Here are the caveats:

- Business social events are not about food and drink. So don't go hungry and don't drink alcohol.

- Do your homework: Remember the 5Ps—Prior Planning Prevents Poor Performance

THE MECHANICS OF BEING A GOOD GUEST

Recognize that, as a guest, you have a role equally as important role as the host's to ensure the success of the occasion. In other words, you'll have to "sing for your supper," and if you do, you will be invited back and included on many other guest lists, giving you the opportunity to make many valuable business contacts. Here are the things you can do to insure that you'll remain on the "A" list.

- Respond as soon as your invitation arrives. Never put it off longer than three or four days.

- Make sure you know what kind of party it is: Holiday celebration? Retirement party? Opening of a new office? To introduce new members of the company? That kind of information will give you important clues as to the nature of the party and how to make the most of it.

- You might consider asking your host who will be there—as long as you've already accepted the invitation (otherwise, it will appear like a condition of acceptance and that's pretty tacky). For example, if the host tells you the entire department will be there, you can say something like, "I've heard you speak of many of them, so I look forward to being able to connect names and faces." That tells your host that you intend to contribute energy to the party, not to be a drain on it.

- Do not arrive even one minute early.

- Arrive no later than 30 minutes after the scheduled arrival time. If you truly are unable to get there until the end, let your host know in advance and explain the reason.

- Do not stay beyond the stated party time, even if other guests do.

- Dress appropriately. If you aren't sure what to wear, ask your host in advance. It's disrespectful to be too casual or overly dressed up.

- Never bring a guest unless your invitation clearly states "and guest." If, for some reason, you must bring a guest (let's say you have an out-of-town friend staying with you), ask your host in advance if it would be OK to bring the guest. Make sure you give the host your guest's name.

- Drink only from glasses. Never drag around a beer bottle or soda can.

- If you are carrying an iced drink, do so with your left hand so you avoid a cold, clammy handshake. A napkin around the glass really doesn't solve the problem. Learn to enjoy drinks that do not have ice in them. Then if you forget and carry the glass in your right hand, there is no harm done.

- Ignore drippy, messy, greasy hors d'oeuvres. They make for unpleasant handshakes.

- Do not pile your plate with food. Gluttony is charm-free. Plus, you'll look sophomoric.

- Make sure you greet your host when you arrive and thank your host when you leave. Don't monopolize their time.

- Drink alcohol in extreme moderation or, better still, not at all. And remember, nobody ever has to apologize for not drinking alcohol.

CIRCULATE, CIRCULATE, CIRCULATE!!!

Remember that everybody has an agenda at a business social event. There is nothing wrong with breaking away from someone by saying, "I'm glad we had some time to catch up. If you'll excuse me, there are a couple of people here I'd like to say hello to before I leave." This is most kindly and effectively done when you can introduce that person to another so he or she isn't suddenly left alone. (See Chapter 10 for more on the art of the introduction.)

- Don't get involved in a deep business conversation. When you've locked on to an arresting topic with someone (perhaps a potential client), say something like, "I'd love to pursue this further. How about if I call and we can have lunch?" Then keep your agreement.

- Smile a lot.

- If you smoke, don't even think about doing so anywhere outside designated areas.

- Send a thank-you note to your host the very next day.

- If you must cancel, say you got called away at the last minute and cannot make the party. Call your host the next morning, explain your emergency, and send flowers. If you are out of town, send a postcard with a written apology.

THE MECHANICS FOR THE HOST

Your job is to assist your guests in having a good time.

Make sure that you have gone over the guest list and are sure how to pronounce each name.

Circulate, circulate, circulate, and introduce people to one another.

Show each guest where to get a drink and some food.

Enlist some assistants as "greeters," especially if it is a large party, to make sure each guest is welcomed at the door, knows where the food is, and has someone to talk to.

Stock up on non-alcoholic drinks so you can be free to ask anyone this simple question: "What would you like to drink?"

If there is some kind of take-away material, to be distributed—a hand-out, for example—make sure the greeters see to that chore.

For more on how to be a host, see the section entitled "The Good Host."

A CLASS ACT KNOWS THAT A GUEST HAS AS MUCH RESPONSIBILITY FOR AN EVENT'S SUCCESS AS THE HOST.

CHAPTER 28

A Class Act Hosts Restaurant Meals Confidently

"No one can worship God or love his neighbor on an empty stomach."
—Woodrow Wilson

THE BUSINESS MEAL

It's a big day. You're taking your boss and her husband to dinner. Or you want to impress a potential big client at a power lunch. Or you just want a quick, quiet dinner by yourself to prepare for a meeting the next morning.

But things don't work out the way you planned.

The Lobster Newburg ordered by your boss's husband turns him into an iceberg when he tastes it. Because you didn't feel comfortable politely negotiating with the waiter who gave him the wrong salad dressing or the stiff maitre d' who gave you the table with the view of the wall, you leave with indigestion, a rocky relationship with the boss, and considerably less money in your pocket.

You didn't land the big client. His steak was overcooked. The wine you selected (without counsel from the maitre d') had no relationship to the food, and your worldly-wise target knows you're bluffing. The deal went sour and the wine might as well have been, too.

Your quick, quiet dinner ended up something like a sitcom. Your waitress turned out to be Roseanne's sister—the rude one—late, loud, and wrong. Wouldn't it have been a good idea to tell her at the outset that you were short on time, or craved solitude and asked her recommendations, rather than visibly and audibly communicating your impatience after the fact?

IT ALL COMES DOWN TO MANNERS

What happened here? Incompetent servers? Brain-damaged managers? Psychotic chefs? Let's look instead at the main cause—bad manners. In a restaurant service situation, the process works like this:

A server, maitre d', and chef are your short-term employees every time you eat in their restaurant. When you exhibit bad manners, your employees are no longer working for you. They're working against you, even though you're still paying the tab. Poorly treated employees produce a poor product. When any of us are treated badly or rudely, we resist. Hence, the person treating us rudely doesn't ever get the full measure of what he wants in the encounter, whether it is cooperation, agreement, or service.

Look at the first example. Although you told the maitre d' that it was a special night when you made the reservation, you did not allow enough time for traffic and arrived a half hour late for your reservation. You then demanded to be seated immediately because you had made a reservation. This strategy just does not work.

In your irritation, you ignored your waiter, who has come to take your drink order while you finished a conversation, thereby invalidating him. You made things worse by ignoring his suggestion that Lobster Newberg might not be the best choice for an entrée. A waiter, in fact, spends an average of just five minutes an evening at a table. It is hardly a major sacrifice to give him your attention when he is there. That creates a win-win situation.

In the second scenario, you're so concerned with impressing a potential client that you completely lost control and reacted by snapping commands at the server, trying to demonstrate who was in charge. The result was that you intimidated him to the point that he made the very mistakes he was trying to avoid.

YOU NEED TO BE IN CONTROL

As in any business situation, dining comes down to the issue of who's in control. An effective host will need to control the entire process. I advocate a dress rehearsal for this very reason. It gives me a measure of control I'd not have otherwise. Even more important than the dress rehearsal is establishing a relationship with one or two restaurants and their staff.

For example, when I go to a new restaurant, I introduce myself to the manager by my name and my company's name. This sends a signal to the restaurant that I'm establishing a business relationship, that I'll be back, and that I'm willing to pay for service. I also discuss the occasion with the maitre d', beforehand if possible, and arrange a corporate billing. This is also the time to get recommendations of wines in your price range. Tip the maitre d' for this advice as you leave. That tip is a wise investment and one that women, in particular, usually forget. And yes, if the maitre d' happens to be a woman, she gets tipped as well.

Even though dining in a nice restaurant should be a pleasurable experience, in the case of a business meal, it also can be a test. You will be observed by your guests on your competency as a CLASS ACT, and you will judge the establishment and its staff as well. It's an opportunity to talk one on one, to demonstrate how you relate to strangers, instruct subordinates, handle utensils, what your taste in food and drink is, and what you like to talk about. That's a lot.

It's easy to be intimidated, especially when most of us no longer learn dining skills at the family dinner table. Today those skills must be learned elsewhere. And those skills must be practiced in order to acquire the confidence to concentrate on the business at hand.

THE CLASS ACT AS HOST

Here are some suggestions to follow when entertaining at a restaurant for business purposes, particularly when you are the host:

- Arrive early, not just on time. Don't order anything or touch the glasses. Everyone in your party should arrive to a pristine table. Leave your napkin on the table until everyone is seated.

- Figure out the seating arrangement ahead of time. The host takes the bad seat, if there is one. This would apply even to a CEO hosting a meeting.

- Let your guests select their menu choices before you make your own. Mention the food the restaurant is noted for. If your budget permits high-end items, like shrimp cocktail, urge your guests to have them.

- Never let a guest eat a course alone. If your guest orders an appetizer, the host should, too. If your guest declines, so should the host. Ditto for dessert, even if it's the moment you've been waiting for all day.

- The server is always looking for cues to suggest who's in charge at the table. Subtle comments to your guests, such as, "Wouldn't you like to check your coat?" indicate that you are the host. Your meal will go more smoothly when you've established that rapport.

- Keep your cool. Just as we make snap judgments about others, snap judgments are being made about us just as often. Perhaps you don't care a whit what your server thinks of you, but a potential client or colleague or boss might be within earshot if you lose your cool over something that could have been avoided.

ANATOMY OF A RESTAURANT

Since most business dining takes place in restaurants, it's useful to understand how restaurants work. The structure of restaurants varies greatly, from a showy Las Vegas-type dining room to a casual California-style eatery to a five-star French haute cuisine establishment. Just as restaurant styles are different, so too is protocol based on each environment.

It's important to understand how a restaurant and its staff operate. Knowing what function each performs, and how they relate to you and each other, will greatly increase your chances of having an enjoyable experience.

Maitre d'/Host/Hostess: The maitre d', who sometimes also is the general manager and in smaller establishments is often the owner, generally is in charge of all floor service. In busier restaurants, the maitre d' will have an assistant manager who helps carry out the many responsibilities of the job. This job includes staffing, coordinating reservations with available seating, timing the flow of patrons to coincide with the pace of the kitchen staff, and handling special requests (like presenting an engagement ring or birthday surprise).

Captain/headwaiter: These terms are interchangeable. Not all restaurants have one. Captains or headwaiters supervise a smaller group of servers. If one person takes your order and another serves, the person who took the order is generally your captain or headwaiter.

Chef: The chef is in charge of the kitchen and its personnel, how food is prepared, presented, and delivered to the table. In larger, busier operations, a chef is a supervisor and not necessarily a cook.

Bartenders and Servers: These are the people who directly serve you.

They are supervised by the maitre d'. Servers include waiters and waitresses and coat-check workers. Servers may also be referred to as waitrons, which is more politically correct but sounds disagreeably like a name for robots. There is also a non-gender specific term.

Bussers and Dishwashers: The busser is usually the first person you see at your table, pouring water and providing bread and butter. Bussers are responsible for clearing dishes after each course, resetting tables, and keeping the dining room stocked with necessary equipment such as china, linen, glassware (or crystal), and silverware. Dishwashers work behind the scenes, cleaning up. You probably won't encounter them. They also are referred to as stewards. Bussers sometimes are referred to as server attendants.

Sommelier: Some restaurants have a sommelier or wine steward. This person orders wine for the restaurant and assists patrons in their wine selection. In most restaurants today, you're most likely to find a maitre d' performing this function.

Each of these employees works to produce one result: a gracious and satisfied customer who will return regularly. But each member is motivated by different needs.

The maitre d' wants everything to run smoothly, efficiently, and profitably. Servers, bartenders, and bussers are motivated by anticipated tips and recognition for a job well done. Chefs are motivated by praise for their taste and creativity. Chefs have a well-earned reputation for being fussy. If you visit one restaurant regularly, it pays to praise the chef, if warranted. It's a good idea to ask for the chef to give personal congratulations or send your message of appreciation through your server.

A Class Act understands and appreciates how restaurants operate.

CHAPTER 29

A Class Act isn't Intimidated by Wine

"A good general rule is to state that the bouquet is better than the taste, and vice versa."

—Stephen Potter (1900-1969), English humorist

Some of life's most challenging purchases are diamonds, furs, and wine. It's also true that we can't impose taste on anyone else—one man's feast is another's famine. Still, when it comes to wine, knowing how to order and serve it goes a long way toward projecting graciousness and savvy.

Many of us are expected to be knowledgeable hosts when we are entertaining clients, and when it comes to picking the right wines there can seem to be an awful lot of pressure brought to bear.

In a restaurant don't be afraid to admit what you don't know! It's perfectly okay to ask the sommelier, maitre d', or server to recommend a wine. That way, there is no risk of embarrassing yourself.

CHOOSING A WINE

Extravagance in the choice of a wine can be seen as gauche and a bad business strategy. Do you want colleagues thinking you are thoughtless with money, or perhaps even worse, lead them into territory where they might not be able to reciprocate? Most good restaurants won't have inferior wines on the list, so opt for the mid-priced bottles.

If you're in a modest restaurant, don't be afraid to order the house wine. And it's never a mistake to choose one bottle and then add orders by the glass if, for example, the majority of the group is drinking a dry burgundy but one person's meal (or preference) just doesn't go well with it. The host should wait until guests have ordered their meals before ordering the wine. Figure on one bottle for three persons, at least. If you are pouring the wine, the glasses should be only half full.

Generally, white wines go with chicken and fish; red ones go with red meats and game. Try a sauvignon blanc for white and pinot noir for red. These are not so overpowering as the standard chardonnay and cabernet sauvignon. They often go well with both fish and meat.

APPROVING THE WINE

Don't be intimidated by this procedure; be confident, ask the waiter if you have a question about the taste, nose, etc. You are in charge and you must approve the wine. Follow these simple guidelines to assure your appearance as a CLASS ACT.

When the wine is presented for your approval, make sure you check the label and be sure it's exactly what you ordered. The server will then open the bottle and present you with the cork. Look at the cork carefully to be sure it's not dried out. That tells you the wine has been stored properly and probably has not turned bad. Pinch it a bit. If it's fine, then lay the cork on the table or give it back to your server and nod. That signals the server to pour the wine.

Don't make a big show of smelling the cork. Cork smells like cork—"eau de tennis shoes." Smelling the cork will not give you any useful information.

The server will pour a small amount of wine in your glass. Taste the wine and nod approval to pour to the server. The server will then pour wine into the guests' glasses first and finally into the host's glass, adding to the small amount poured earlier to taste.

AT HOME

Show the label to your guests if you are proud of the wine. If the wine is nothing to shout about, and you are entertaining at home, then present it in a nice decanter or carafe. Wine bottles should be placed on a wine coaster so they don't mark the table.

Most red wines should be served at a cool room temperature. White wines should be chilled at least two hours in the refrigerator before serving. You'll never go wrong holding a wine glass by its stem. It's fine to hold red wines by the bowl of the glass, because the heat from your hand often improves the flavor and bouquet of the wine.

As host, you would serve guests around the table the first time. Start with the person at your right, and finish with yourself after you've gone around the table. After that, ask someone at the other end of the table to take on the job to make things simpler.

Always change a guest's glass when a different wine is poured. In other words, don't pour white wine into a glass that just held red wine. Don't be afraid to hold a napkin under the neck of the bottle to catch drips. Those baskets that hold wine sideways are designed to catch the wine's sediment at the bottom of the bottle.

THERE'S ALWAYS MORE TO LEARN

Some wonderful books that can teach you more about wine are the *Windows on the World Complete Wine Course* and *The Wall Street Journal Guide to Wine*. Seek out good wine merchants and pick their brains—you learn most through discussion and experience.

A CLASS ACT APPRECIATES WINE, KNOWS HOW TO SELECT, POUR, AND DRINK IT—YET IS NOT EMBARASSED TO SAY WHAT HE DOESN'T KNOW.

CHAPTER 30

A Class Act Knows How (and When) to Drink with Colleagues

"Work is the curse of the drinking classes."

—Oscar Wilde

Whether you're a drinker or a health-conscious teetotaler, here are some face-saving tips about how to behave at work-related cocktail parties or when you're down at the corner bistro after a long day at the office.

IT SEEMS SO SIMPLE, BUT . . .

You and a colleague, perhaps your boss, have arranged to meet for drinks at a restaurant or sports bar. Or perhaps you are on your way to a business cocktail party. In both cases, drinking dilemmas will have their day.

What to order? How many is too much? Does sitting at a cocktail table for two suggest an intimacy you'd prefer to avoid? Does standing at the bar suggest a "hail fellow, well met!" image you'd rather not project?

Meeting for drinks may have been your bright idea—what if the other person doesn't drink at all?

NO ONE EVER *HAS* TO DRINK

Remember this: a person never has to apologize for not drinking alcohol. Ever.

All you have to say is, "I'm not having wine/beer/liquor today. Please go ahead and enjoy whatever you want. I'm perfectly happy."

This statement, utilizing the word "today," removes any judgment about the consumption of alcohol. You don't even need to drink alcohol when you propose a toast. Be decisive about your order, especially if you don't drink. Mention your beverage of choice by name.

"I'll have a Pellegrino with a twist, please," for example. That just sounds a lot more savvy than muttering, "Oh, I'll just have a glass of water."

STICK TO THE TWO-DRINK LIMIT

Two drinks should be the limit when you're imbibing alcohol, whether it's wine, beer, or liquor. For that matter, stick to the two-drink rule when you're drinking just about anything. Otherwise, your lingering might be misconstrued.

If you are standing at the bar, which is preferable to a dark table in the corner (which also might be misconstrued), start a tab. Close it when you've hit your limit of two. Say to your companion, "Will you do the math, or should I?" Then settle the check and leave. The entire encounter shouldn't last longer than an hour at the outside.

BE YOURSELF

Drinks with business associates is no time to experiment with exotic concoctions, nor is it the moment to have your first martini (take it from one who knows!) dry with a twist.

Be authentic—and low maintenance. If all you ever drink is Diet Pepsi, don't stop now. If you're a beer-on-tap person, keep on keeping on. Wine drinkers gain nothing by pretending phony sophistication, especially when the choice is house white or house red.

Unless the house choices happen to be Cuvee Rot Gut, drink them and don't interrogate bartenders who are doing their best to serve 50 people at once. Most decent restaurants and bars serve quality house brands. If they carry a premium choice, they'll tell you. Don't be afraid or shy to ask what it costs if the server doesn't volunteer it. And once told, don't be too intimidated to decline on the basis of price. That shows you're secure; not cheap.

USE YOUR HEAD

Know your limits. If you're sleep-deprived and stressed out, chances are that one alcoholic drink will hit you faster than when you're on vacation.

Don't ever drink on an empty stomach. Eat an apple, a sandwich, granola bar, anything, before you add alcohol. The single worst gaffe you can make is to get loaded, regardless of how much others try to goad you into excess.

Should an associate's sobriety come into question, don't hesitate to take him or her home by cab. Be firm and unemotional, "I'd feel a lot better if we get into a cab and drop you off." If that should happen to be your boss, never mention it unless he or she does first. And never speak of it with anyone else.

Should you be the one who needed to be driven home, apologize the next day and never again speak of it, especially not in jest. Keep in mind that, whatever the venue, you are still at a business meeting. As such, you cannot afford to let down your guard again. If you do, the price might be impossibly high.

Cheers!

A CLASS ACT NEVER ABUSES ALCOHOL.

Part VII

THE CLASS ACT IS A GRACIOUS HOST

Business entertaining is not just about food and socializing. In fact, it would be wise to think of business entertaining as an opportunity to spotlight your social skills and your level of sophistication.

How can you be sure that you are a CLASS ACT as a host when engaged in business entertaining? The key is preparation so that your social event will accomplish its purposes and reflect well on you. This section will provide you with all the information and insights you need to succeed when you are entertaining in the world of business.

CHAPTER 31

A Class Act Entertains at Home

"'Mid pleasures and palaces though we may roam, Be it ever so humble, there's no place like home."

—John Howard Payne

Years of apathy and lack of participation dissolved in the course of one summer afternoon. The executive committee of our local chapter of the Society of Professional Journalists had been inattentive at best, meeting in a Chinese restaurant every month to develop compelling events and raise funds for the scholarship program. Interest waned and our numbers dwindled. Then Patti Mengers took the lead.

As the newly elected president of our merry band, she called her first meeting at her home—in August. On a Saturday afternoon. There were sandwiches, muffins, shrimp cocktail, cheese, fruit, wine, iced tea, and soft drinks—all picked up that morning from the neighborhood deli. It could not have been simpler or more charming. We sat in her city garden and ideas and energy flowed.

What was the elixir that changed the energy and dedication of the group?

THE BEST PLACE TO DO BUSINESS

It was being in Patti's home. Yet again, it was an example that our home is the best place to do business entertaining. We all are so time-crunched and on the go that sharing someone's home is very special and could not be more flattering, especially for businesspeople like myself, who seem always to be in cars, trains, planes, and hotels.

Yet the thought of entertaining at home usually strikes fear in the most confident of hearts. Too many people cheat themselves out of the gift of bringing people together for good conversation and good food by telling themselves they can't entertain. Panic grips their heart. They will be judged. They will be found wanting. It will be a mess. They can't possibly get everything ready. It is all too much, too much, too . . .

Let's get a grip right now. Remember: the only true gifts we can give are our time and attention. Nothing says that more eloquently than sharing our home with others. You don't have to be the next Julia Child with a house like Martha Stewart's to entertain successfully. It has nothing to do with how much furniture you have or how much money you are able to spend. You do not have to impress people with what you have, and you never have to apologize for what you do not have.

START WITH A SMALL SOIREE

The best way to get over your worries about entertaining is just to go ahead and give a party. Start small. Most people are so pleased to be invited to someone's home that the size of the party doesn't matter. One of my most pleasant memories is of my neighbor's annual holiday dessert get-together. Several of her colleagues and friends gathered at her house for after-dinner desserts, all purchased from nearby pastry shops and served with so much warmth and grace that we all felt very special. The fire was roaring, the candles were flickering, the coffee and cordials were warming. She was a working mother with more chores than time, yet these small, uncomplicated gatherings were always successful.

Shortcuts go a long way in home entertaining. Invite people over for drinks before going to dinner—or for dessert and coffee afterwards. You will infuse the occasion with your energy and warmth—minus a lot of the trouble of an entire meal. Should some of your guests travel a long way to be there, of course, a meal is a must.

A party—or any gathering—is only as good as its guests. Who invites whom?

And to what?

Not every person or situation calls for an invitation to your home. For example, if you have a strictly business relationship with colleagues, invite them to lunch in a restaurant.

Invite a business colleague who has become a friend, with a date or spouse, to dinner in your home or at a restaurant. Invitations to a social dinner or weekend event should include spouses. A midweek lunch doesn't require spouses be invited. It's not appropriate for two people married to others to dine alone together at dinner. If your out-of-town business colleague shows up with a spouse, invite the couple to dinner with your spouse or a co-host.

Some Points to Consider When You're Entertaining at Home

Make sure guests understand how to get to your home. E-mail explicit directions or include a map and directions with your mailed invitation. Don't expect them to look it up on the Internet or to call AAA for a trip map.

Arrange to pick up your guest of honor or someone elderly if you live in the country. Another guest can call for them, or hire a car service. If parking is difficult at your home, consider hiring a valet service.

Make sure you have enough seating space for guests to dine comfortably. Hiring a good caterer is a wise investment for a formal dinner party. They can provide staff to help serve and clear.

At an informal dinner at home, things are different. Still, make sure you provide a meal—never invite someone to dinner and then serve snacks instead. Use real flatware and china—casual dining at home does not equate to plastic, unless it's poolside. Use cloth napkins. Make sure you have soft drinks as well as wine or cocktails on hand. Decline your guest's offers to help you with the dishes—that usually creates confusion. Spoil your guests! Make sure your children are introduced. You might even press them into passing hors d'oeuvres. But don't have them participate in the meal. That's tedious for both the children and your guests.

It's true that "God is in the details," and it's never more true than when you're giving a large business meal at your home. You'll need an aide-de-camp unless you can devote most of your time to the project. He or she should be resourceful, detail-driven, and able to deal with people effectively. Your job and your co-host's job, whether it's your spouse, significant other, or a date, is to pay attention to the guests. Thus, division of labor makes sense.

Here are some of the details to nail down: Develop guest list. Invitations—design, produce, and mail. Flowers. Coordinate with the caterer. Menu cards and place cards produced and placed. Greet guests, check them in, and direct them where to leave coats. Handle all incoming telephone calls during the party, as well as call guests who are absent or late. Coordinate entertainers if there are any. Show any staff where to dress, and get refreshments for themselves. Pay everyone at party's end.

The caterer is responsible for hiring the appropriate staff, preparing the food, stocking the bar (even if the host provides the alcohol), bringing rental equipment for anything missing in the house, providing ice and cocktail napkins, organizing facilities to check coats, hiring and supervising valet parking, serving the meal after cocktails, and serving after-dinner drinks. Finally, the caterer should clean up everything concerning the party as well as putting back furniture that had to be moved to accommodate the guests.

THE GUEST LIST

Making up the guest list always is a challenge and the most critical part of any gathering. The secret's in the mix of people. Think of a party as an opportunity to bring together people who don't know each other but who probably will enjoy meeting one another. It's an opportunity to bring together old friends who never seem to have enough time to visit with one another. Invite people who will appreciate the invitation and will make an effort to contribute to the success of the party.

Don't invite just one type of person. A room full of only lawyers or doctors is antithetical to the very idea of a party. Don't throw in a person or couple who really don't fit the group just because you owe them a dinner. Don't invite known adversaries on the theory that it will make the party livelier. It may make the party livelier than you had hoped.

Everybody has their own little tricks and preferences when it comes to making up a great guest list. My personal formula, for example, always includes:

- A banker, because they know a little about a lot of industries and can talk about what's going on in the economy.

- A journalist, because they ask great questions.

- Somebody involved in politics, however tangentially.

- A restaurateur, because the entire world is interested in dining out and in food.

- Someone in marketing, because they usually have something interesting to say about trends, tastes, and what people are buying.

SEATING LOGIC

The reason seating is so important is that it provides you the host with the opportunity to thoughtfully orchestrate connections, establish relationships, and provide good company at the beginning.

The Seat of Honor Goes to:

- Foreign guest

- Someone visiting you

- Elderly

- Distinguished Career

- Formerly held appointment, elected office, or military rank

- Celebrating birthday, anniversary, a promotion

Rules of Thumb for Correct Seating:

- Non-ranked should alternate when possible

- Spouses should not be seated next to each other

- Unmarried couples may or may not sit next to each other

- Spouses should be seated at different tables, if possible

- Large function: seat a young person next to an older one, but also seat a young person nearer this person's own age on the other side

- A guest from a foreign country should be seated near a colleague who has done business in that country

- Guests who don't know each other but share passionate interests should be seated together

- Seat a shy person next to a talkative one

- The spouse with the higher position and title should be given the better seat

- Be sure to mix the best conversationalists throughout the seating arrangement.

WAYS TO HEAD OFF POTENTIAL DISASTER WITH CLASS

1. **One of your guests hasn't arrived, and it's time to serve dinner.** Serve the dinner on time, even if it's your guest of honor who is late. Keep in mind the well-being of the group. When the latecomer arrives, he should join the meal with whatever course happens to be served. Don't try to make up for lost time by serving soup when everybody else is on his or her entrée. Everybody will survive and be grateful for your presence of mind.

2. **Your guests won't leave.** Take action! Nothing is worse than a couple of stragglers who seem intent on having yet another drink. Stand up and say something like, "With the brain-trust that we have here tonight, the business world won't survive tomorrow unless we all get some sleep! Thank you so much for spending time with us here. It's been a wonderful evening." Yes, you are throwing them out. With good humor, you not only will get away with it—the other guests (who really want to leave) will thank you.

   If you have a guest of honor, protocol dictates that the guests cannot leave until he or she does. If you must clue this person in, do it privately. It might sound like, "Mr. Thomas, I believe the others are waiting for the guest of honor before they leave." No business dinner party should go on beyond 11 P.M. Experienced guests who are guests of honor know this.

3. **Refusing an unexpected guest or a last-minute addition.** If you can

accommodate the extra person without undue disruption, do so gracefully and as cheerfully as possible. However, there are situations in which you should refuse to accept the added guest. It may be that adding a seemingly discordant plate or flatware to your perfectly set table would just make you crazy, or you can't just fabricate a seventh Cornish game hen if you have planned to feed six people. The refusal should not be insulting and should be accomplished with as much grace and good humor as possible. One reputedly excellent hostess used to call on me regularly to attend her seated dinner parties. One day, when she called to invite me to dinner, I told her that I had gotten married a month before. "That's terrible," she said. "You can't bring your husband. It will ruin my seating arrangement!" Happily, I never heard from her again.

4. **Your guests are taking sides on an issue and it could get ugly. What do you say?** Anything. If you are giving a party, always be ready with a store of anecdotes or comments about something in the news that will change the subject. If this fails, propose a toast to something or somebody. The point is to steer the conversation onto another subject.

THE RULES OF RECIPROCITY

You must reciprocate when you have been taken to a business or socially oriented meal.

"Never lead a person where they cannot follow," as the saying goes. It's unkind and inconsiderate to entertain at a level that others cannot match. Reciprocating becomes embarrassing. If both spouses work and you are inviting another dual-career couple to dinner, the husband or wife who knows the spouse of the other couple should extend the invitation.

A CLASS ACT WELCOMES GUESTS TO HER HOME—AND MAKES THEM FEEL WELCOME THERE.

CHAPTER 32

The Class Act Entertains in Restaurants

"A host is like a general: calamities often reveal his genius."
—Horace

THE IMPORTANCE OF THE VENUE

Think about the purpose of the event, the mixture of guests, the level of expense which is appropriate, and the comfort of the group. You will start off on a Class Act footing if you are prepared to select the most appropriate venue.

CHOOSING A RESTAURANT

Keep these two guidelines in mind as you select your restaurant:

- **Don't experiment.** Select a restaurant you know very well or "scout" some good, convenient places several times to become familiar with the dining room, the menu, and management.

- **Watch costs.** Choose a quality restaurant with reliable service. Don't skimp, but don't overspend. Extravagance shows bad manners and poor judgment.

ISSUING INVITATIONS

Here are some tips for issuing invitations:

- Make the calls to invite people yourself; do not have an assistant make them.

- Call the most important person first or the hardest person to pin down.

- Include in your call your reason for the business meeting.

- Tell the person the names of the other people you are inviting.

- Give the first person you call two choices of days and restaurants.

- Ask if they prefer smoking or non-smoking.

- Confirm the time and place as you conclude the call.

- Confirm again before the meeting. If it's at breakfast, confirm the afternoon beforehand. For lunch or dinner, confirm the day before.

- Give your guests your home number and the number of the restaurant in case an emergency arises.

DRESS REHEARSAL

As the director of the event you are planning, allow time for a dress rehearsal that will include surveying the "stage" at the restaurant.

- Visit the restaurant in advance of the meeting, preferably at meal-time.

- Look for a table in a good position—a corner spot or one a little distance from other tables.

- Reserve the table you pick.

- Speak with the maitre d' or manager. Make the reservation in your name and in the name of your company, and give the restaurant staff the message that this is an important business meeting.

- Set up a corporate account or allow them to make a credit card imprint.

- Inquire about ordering wine, the price range, and ask for suggestions.

- Tip the maitre d', if he is the one with whom you've spoken; $10 to $20 is appropriate, depending on the restaurant.

YOUR ROLE AS HOST

Arrive ten minutes before your guests. Tip the maitre d' if you haven't done so already. Wait near the door for your guests if possible. If you must wait at the table, do not eat or drink anything or disturb the table setting.

Stand up and greet your guests as they arrive. Shake the hand of all your guests or if that is impossible then acknowledge them with a gesture. Remain standing until everyone is seated. If someone leaves the table during the meal, it is not necessary to stand.

Don't set up shop on the table. Try to adhere to the rule that, "if it isn't part of the meal, it shouldn't be on the table."

Turn off your cell phone unless you explain to your guests in advance that you must take an urgent call if it comes in during the meal.

SUBTLY CONTROL THE SEATING ORDER

Encourage people to sit where you want them to by asking them politely or by pointing to or touching a chair. Try to have the principal guest or guests sitting at right angles to you or across from you.

ORDERING DRINKS

Just a few suggestions for ordering drinks:

- Let your guests reply first when the server asks if anyone wants something from the bar.

- If they do not order drinks, neither do you.

- It's fine to order something non-alcoholic when they order alcohol, but you might want to make your guests more comfortable by saying, "I'm not having a drink today, just some club soda." This "today" makes it clear you do not disapprove of your guests' drinking.

- If no drinks are ordered, engage in minor conversation for a few minutes before ordering.

- If there are drinks, the server will return to ask about refills. If the answer is no, ask for menus. If the answer is yes, ask for menus when the second round arrives.

ORDERING DINNER

Simple steps to remember at this stage:

- Your homework comes into play here. You can make recommendations and encourage guests to order appetizers.

- Stop talking, look at the menu, make a decision, put the menu down.

- Consider ordering user-friendly food.

- Have the server take the guests' orders first.

- Order the same number of courses as they do.

SELECTING THE WINE

If your guests indicate they would enjoy wine with the meal, pick a mid-priced bottle, or, in a modest restaurant, the house wine.

One bottle for three people. A sauvignon blanc (white) and pinot noir (red) go well with both fish and meat and are not overpowering.

When the server presents the bottle of wine, check the label to be sure it is what you ordered. The server will open the bottle and present you with the cork. Pinch it to make sure it is not dried out. Lay it on the table or give it back to the waiter. This is the signal to pour.

Taste the small amount poured for you and nod your approval. Your guests will be served first.

WHEN TO TALK BUSINESS, AND DESSERT

Encourage everyone to have dessert and make recommendations. Follow their lead, whether you want dessert or not. Ask if they would like coffee or tea; when it is served, ask for the check.

While you may have covered your agenda throughout the meal, now is a critical time for you to review what has been discussed and perhaps summarize what still must be decided. Make sure everyone knows the outcome of this meeting and if another is planned.

Now is the time to write things down and, if needed, give people material to take away from the meeting.

PAYING, TIPPING, AND LEAVING

As the actors prepare to leave the stage, you, as director, see that the "play" concludes happily and smoothly. Here are some ways to ensure that:

- Review the bill briefly, and if there is a problem with it, take it up after the guests have left.

- If a guest starts haggling over the bill, just say pleasantly, "I invited you—and besides, my company would like to buy you lunch."

- Make sure your previous arrangement for paying the bill (company account or credit-card imprint) included an 18 to 20 percent tip for the server. The captain or head waiter gets 5 percent of the bill in cash. The sommelier or wine steward gets 15 percent of the wine bill if he helped you make a selection. The maitre d', if not tipped beforehand, gets $10 to $20 in cash.

- Collect checkroom tickets from your guests on the way out and pay the attendant $1 per garment.

- Escort your guests to the door. Shake hands and thank them for joining you. Apologize if there was any problem with food or service.

- Remind them about the next meeting, if there will be one, or tell them you'll be contacting them to set one up.

- After they have left, make some notes if needed, and congratulate yourself on a job well done.

A CLASS ACT KNOWS HOW TO ENTERTAIN ADVANTAGEOUSLY IN RESTAURANTS, WITH GRACIOUS CIVILITY.

CHAPTER 33

A Class Act Entertains at a Private Club

"London clubs remain insistent on keeping people out, long after they have stopped wanting to come in."

—Anthony Sampson

THE ETIQUETTE OF CLUBS

Private clubs each present their own set of etiquette rules. Whether it's your club or you're using someone else's membership, the beauty is that the club sort of becomes a home away from home. The service is usually excellent, and the food and facilities are very good, too. There are four basic kinds of private clubs: eating-only clubs, sports and eating clubs, business-oriented clubs, and social clubs.

SOCIAL CLUB

If you are in a social club, overt acts of "doing business" are normally not permitted, because such clubs undoubtedly enjoy a tax-exempt status. In other words, the club doesn't make any profit. Technically, you're not supposed to even meet a business contact there for lunch if you intend to discuss business. I'm certain that members often do talk business. However, bringing out papers, opening briefcases, and so forth will call attention to

business interactions. So the club management is forced to request that it be stopped. The by-laws of social clubs usually forbid companies to pay dues; members must pay them personally.

PRIVATE CLUB

As a host in a private club, make sure your guests understand the nature of the club. If it's a purely social club, make it clear that any business talk will be low-key at best. Telling them about the dress code when you invite them will help to prevent any embarrassment.

When I lived in Egypt, for instance, the tennis club strictly forbade any color other than white on the courts. Some clubs still adhere to this. Many clubs require jacket and tie for men in the dining room. In general, conservative dress is the norm. That means no skin-baring attire for women. Evening activities usually call for traditional business attire, unless an event is designated as black tie.

Never roam around a private club on your own. If your host hasn't arrived to meet you, the doorman will direct you to the lobby or waiting area. Stay there until your host shows up. Then you can ask for a tour of the premises, which often are filled with fascinating memorabilia portraits of prominent members, historical furniture, and rare books. Members love to tell their stories, so don't be shy about asking. Some clubs even provide printed histories to accommodate these requests.

Be sure to explain the club's tipping policy to your guests. Many clubs forbid tipping anyone, including coat check personnel, restroom attendants, caddies, housekeepers, waiters, and waitresses. Accepting a tip might cost club employees their job, so be sure to make the policy clear. It is, however, perfectly acceptable to send a check made out to the club's holiday fund to express your appreciation.

Although you might want to pick up the meal tab, private clubs do not accept cash. Members usually receive a bill each month for restaurant and bar charges.

AT YOUR BOSS'S CLUB

Should your boss request you to entertain at her club, remember that your behavior reflects on her, the member. That means it's doubly important that no one drinks too much and becomes disorderly. On the positive side, it will be quite easy to make whatever arrangements you need. The club will accord you the same courtesy and service as they would your sponsoring member. Deal with the club personnel as you would a banquet manager in a fine hotel. Take great care to pay the bill the minute your sponsor receives it. That bill will include the club's standard gratuity charge. By all means give a contribution to the club's holiday fund if your event was successful. A letter to the club's president should accompany this. Not only will it be shown around and thus boost everyone's morale at the club; your letter will serve as an insurance policy for excellent service in the future.

Of course, your boss should not expect you to entertain for business if her club is purely social. And you never should request to use it for business purposes. Before asking anyone to sponsor your entertaining at their private club, remember that it is a very big favor to do so. Don't take it personally if they turn you down; sometimes the club requires the sponsoring member to attend the function. And of course, many club members have been burned by well-meaning friends who abuse the privilege.

A CLASS ACT UNDERSTANDS THE PRIVILEGE AND CONVENIENCE OF PRIVATE CLUBS AND NEVER ABUSES THEM.

Part VIII

THE CIRCLE OF LIFE

CHAPTER 34

A Class Act Celebrates the Passages of Life

"Sunrise, sunset . . . Swiftly go the years."

—*Fiddler on the Roof*

Births, christenings, coming-of-age ceremonies, birthdays, retirements, engagements, weddings, funerals. These are the milestones of our lives. A Class Act observes such milestones with thoughtful attention and appropriate celebration.

Each milestone represents one door closing and another door opening. Each is a time of community, a time when we depend on each other to share our excitement, our joy, our anxiety, our sadness. Each is a time to support one another even though we might be "just colleagues" and only tangentially involved in each event or we may or may not be invited to participate directly in the occasions. Still, these are eminently human occurrences, filled with emotion and import, and it's only kind to recognize them and acknowledge them. The truth is that all of us depend on each other and take comfort in the goodwill and camaraderie we extend toward one another. The best way to do this is by celebrating key events in each others' lives. When co-workers are happy and care about one another, it helps to foster the teamwork that is essential for success.

When such events take place the lines blur between personal and professional life. Here are some guidelines for respectfully and appropriately

commemorating life events when they happen in the workplace. These guidelines are important because they help us to express our good wishes in a professional manner. The joke gift and funny card you give a close friend or relative will not be appropriate for your boss, subordinate, or co-worker.

GIFTS VS. CARDS

In fact, the question of gift giving is always a relevant issue, whether you actually attend the celebration or not. But, generally, a gift is not necessary unless you actually attend the celebration as an invited guest. To be sure you understand the rules of gift giving, see Chapter 19 for more detailed information.

One thing you must do, however, is to acknowledge the event (this is true even if giving a gift is not appropriate).

Handwritten notes—not prepackaged-sentiment cards—are the best way to go and are always appreciated. These personally written messages, especially those written from the heart, sometimes can function as the gift and are often treasured long after the event. (See Chapter 15 for more on the power of hand-written correspondence.)

ENGAGEMENTS

These days it's common to celebrate the wedding engagement of a co-worker. Most of the time, someone will be in charge of buying a gift and may ask everyone to contribute money toward the purchase.

If that is not the case, simply write a note giving your own good wishes. All it takes are a few minutes to mention how happy you are for the couple and how you wish them a wonderful, happy and healthy life together. Having done that, you are not under any obligation to bring a gift to an engagement party. If you do, it can be something very modest, such as a small picture frame.

BRIDAL SHOWERS

Bridal showers never should be held at the office, because such an event is a truly personal celebration and, as such, is not a "business related" event. If you are an executive and an important client or customer gets married, consider purchasing a significant gift, even if you do not attend the wedding. This, however, is not mandatory and only should occur if a friendship exists between you. Check to see if your company has a policy on such matters—and a gift fund.

WEDDINGS

There are no definite rules for whether to invite a supervisor to your wedding. That depends on the size and culture of the company and your relationship with the supervisor. Some companies approve of socializing; others frown on it. Still, no employee is obligated to invite his or her superior to the wedding. And no boss is obligated to attend any employee's wedding.

It's a courtesy to invite your supervisor if you have a warm relationship. In turn, the supervisor should have a policy about weddings and gifts and be consistent about it. It's gracious and intelligent to send a subordinate a small gift such as a picture frame even if you don't attend the wedding. Be certain to give the same kind of gift to all your subordinates.

BIRTHS

Although it's not necessary to send a baby gift to a supervisor, a subordinate, or a co-worker, you should, however, send a personal note of congratulations to both parents. It might sound like, "Perhaps the best, happiest news of this quarterly report is the arrival of _____. And the best news for him/her is that he/she has you for parents. I send you congratulations and blessings for your continued joy and good health."

CHRISTENINGS, BAR MITZVAHS, AND BAT MITZVAHS

It is an honor to be invited to such an event. There is no rule that says you must accept an invitation, but if you do, however, you must send a gift. It's very thoughtful to send a small gift whether or not you attend. Send a note of congratulations to the child if you know him or her, or to the parents.

BIRTHDAYS

Do everyone a favor. Keep birthday celebrations out of the workplace. They take up time and ultimately cost goodwill from supervisors. And it's nearly impossible to maintain a crumb-free workspace. If a work-friend is having one, arrange a lunch out or a dinner outside the workplace to celebrate. It's best to keep gift giving on a personal level. If you want to give a gift to a work friend, do it in private.

Birthday cards are another story. People enjoy having their special day acknowledged. It's kind to send a birthday card with a note that recounts some of the best moments of the past year and looks forward to the coming one. That might sound like, "You've had quite a year—learned to ski, took up yoga, had a baby, and brought in record sales figures. I can hardly wait to see what you do for encores next year! Meanwhile, I send you warm wishes for your continued health, energy, and success."

RETIREMENT

Most companies have policies that govern the type of celebration to take place. This usually depends on the rank of the employee. Here a "Company Gift" will be bestowed on the retiree. Even in these cases, if the retiree is someone you are friendly with, it's gracious to commemorate the occasion with a card or an upbeat letter that focuses on the future. Many retirees are much younger than those of the past; thus, the emphasis often is on what life adventure will be next.

Gifts are appropriate if you and the retiree are friends, and it's gracious to include the retiree's life partner in gifts—perhaps a gift certificate for a wonderful dinner. If the retiree is the traditional age and has spent decades with your company, it's especially important not to patronize. It's a difficult time in the best of all worlds. Younger colleagues can create a real win-win when they take the time to get to know an older retiree and pick his or her brain about life and work. The retiree will feel valued, and the younger colleague will gain invaluable insights, information, and knowledge. Transitions are never easy, and retiring, in particular, should be treated sensitively. Forget sophomoric questions or jokes to spouses like "what will you do with each other every day?"

A CLASS ACT KNOWS THE RULES FOR APPROPRIATE CELEBRATION
OF EVENTS, BOTH PERSONALLY AND IN A BUSINESS SETTING.

CHAPTER 35

A Class Act Understands the Etiquette
of Condolence

*"I didn't attend the funeral, but I sent a nice letter saying that I approved
of it."*

—Mark Twain

In matters of life and death, we're all vulnerable and needy, and grateful
for any gesture. Never let your own discomfort about death stop you from
consoling the bereaved.

I stared at the puppy as if it were an exotic life form. A high-school friend
I hadn't seen in twenty years was offering it to me. "I thought a warm, furry
friend was just what you need right now."

I was standing in a reception line in a funeral home trying to get through
my mother's viewing. I was already shell-shocked and lost. That well-intentioned "gift" stunned me into near-speechlessness, but I managed to thank
her politely and also convince her that it was in the puppy's best interest to
be placed elsewhere. That was a situation for which nothing in all my years
of advising and counseling about etiquette had prepared me.

Experiencing my mother's death and all the sometimes agonizing, sometimes uplifting events in the days that followed taught me a great many lessons and also altered my ideas about the etiquette of bereavement.

Most of all, I learned that the "wrong" thing to do is nothing. Everything else is right.

Two vignettes follow which illustrate the thoughtful sensitivity required in such situations.

BOTH OF US WERE IN THE WRONG

A young woman I had mentored, and was quite fond of, left a breezy telephone message about how busy she was, and how well life was treating her. But she failed to mention my mom's death, although I was sure she knew about it.

My anger flared. I called back and left a message of my own: "It was good to hear from you, but my mother just died. You knew it, and you didn't even bother to mention it." Her response was to make the hour drive to my home to drop off a written apology. In her note, she told me that the idea of death made her uncomfortable, and she didn't know what to say.

Later, I realized that she didn't think of me, her mentor, as a person in need of help and consolation. But in matters of life and death, we're all vulnerable and needy, and grateful for any gesture recognizing our grief, however faltering.

A COLD-HEARTED RATIONALIZER

A waitress overheard my friend and me making plans to bring dinner to another pal who'd just lost his mother. The waitress interrupted, saying, "I always figure that when you do something like that, you end up creating one more thing for the person to do, because they feel they must send a thank-you note." She preferred to do nothing, she said, out of consideration to the bereaved.

But good manners are about kindness. In order to be kind to someone bereaved, you should make an attempt to acknowledge their sorrow. It's not difficult.

WHAT TO SAY AND HOW TO SAY IT

Here's a primer on how to be kind to someone who has lost a loved one:

- Not knowing what to say is no excuse for remaining silent. It doesn't matter what you say. Most of us waste precious time and cause ourselves needless anxiety wondering about how to talk to a person who has just suffered the loss of a loved one. My best advice is to remember that the reason you are putting yourself through all this wondering about what may be the right thing to say is because you care about the bereaved person. Ironically, this caring should make your condolences easier to speak. You can simply say, "I am so very sorry about your loss." Make eye contact. If you have fond memories, that's the time to relate them. "I still remember all her goofy Halloween costumes and decorations. She was more of a kid than we were at the time," one childhood friend reminded me, and I loved her for that.

    In a business relationship, acknowledging a person's loss shows that you care. Death is difficult for everyone, so don't deprive someone of your support simply because you are uncomfortable. Here are some guidelines to help you.

- Don't be afraid to say the deceased person's name or to say the word "death." These words won't cause any more pain than the bereaved is already feeling.

- Speak to all the family members, not just the ones you know. Introduce yourself and explain your relationship. That might sound like, "I'm Mary Mitchell. I went to grade school with Kathleen, and we've remained close all these years, mostly because we have such good memories of being part of each other's family." Or, "I'm Mary Mitchell. I worked in the same department with Mr. Spade for seven years and I'll miss him. Our whole department will." Don't forget to address children, too. Sometimes young people who lose a loved one would give anything to hear other people's memories of their loved one.

- Don't be afraid of laughing when you're sharing happy memories. Laughter doesn't show disrespect for the dead. In fact, it can express joy at having known a person in a way that words cannot.

- Say something personal and positive. Refer to the person's achievements, even if it's something as simple as baking great chocolate cake. If you never met the person who died, say something like, "I am sorry that I never met your mom, because I remember the wonderful stories you told me about her."

- If you don't know what to say, be honest and say so. "I'm Mary Mitchell. I am so sorry about Jack's death. It came as such a shock, I just don't know what to say. I am just so sorry for your loss."

- Be ready to listen. Your simple condolence might evoke a stream of memories from the bereaved. They might tell you things that wouldn't ordinarily be shared. Don't expect the bereaved to make sense and don't embarrass them by attempting to tie loose ends or to get facts straight. Just listen.

- Don't be afraid to touch. Take a person's hand. Hug people. If they shrink from you, let go. If they dissolve into tears, hang on.

- Go to the service if you can, even if you're busy. There's no substitute for your physical presence. When you look out at the church full of people, it helps to see so many friends and loved ones cherishing the memory of the deceased. I knew lots of people loved my mom and that really helped me get through it.

- Do the write thing. When someone's part of the everyday fabric of your life, an e-mail takes advantage of the immediacy of the medium. However, handwritten letters become part of a person's family history. Letters are permanent, they are always there to share with our children when they're old enough to read and understand. It's a way of extending the memory of someone we loved.

- Remember that a condolence letter is meant for the recipient, not the sender. Don't write about yourself by saying things like, "I am so sorry to hear the news of your mom's death. I often wonder how I myself will react when faced with the same circumstance." A condolence is written to comfort others, not have them feel sorry for you.

- I often close a letter of condolence by suggesting that the healing from grief is made easier when we focus on loving those who are still with us a bit more, compassionately and thoughtfully.

- Send good photographs of the deceased. You may help grief-stricken relatives remember an event that will comfort them in this time of need.

- Help with chores. Bring food. Walk pets. Get the car washed. Offer to keep a record of the letters and gifts so the bereaved can thank everyone. Volunteer to make room reservations for out-of-town guests. If you have expertise in an area, offer it. That will leave family members free to concentrate on what they need to do—grieve.

- Follow through on your offers and promises. Don't promise or offer to do things you can't deliver. If you've said you'd call, then call. If you think you've let too much time go by, believe me, you haven't. One friend of mine asked me shortly after Mom died what she could do. I told her that I'd really like just to go to dinner and tell Mom stories together. She followed through a year later, and it was wonderful.

- In time, check in with the bereaved. A simple call to say, "I was just thinking about you. How are you doing?" can mean so much. Remember that weekends can be lonely for the half of a couple left behind. Be specific. That might sound like, "I just saw an ad for a crafts fair and thought you'd like to join me. Is it okay if I pick you up at 2?" Don't isolate the friend. It's fine to ask, "Is it too painful for you to hear my anecdotes about your dad?" Remember that holidays can be miserable.

- Remember the deceased's birthday in years to come as well as acknowledging the difficulty of holidays and anniversaries. In fact, sometimes reaching out after time has passed is more comforting than during grieving shortly after the death.

In all of this, remember that you're dealing with a person who's damaged—someone who might feel like a survivor who walks away physically unscathed from a car crash. They may not be injured, but they're dazed and disconnected in places doctors can't touch.

A CLASS ACT IS A SURVIVOR WHO UNDERSTANDS THAT THIS IS THE TIME TO REACH OUT IN SOME WAY TO EXPRESS SYMPATHY AND SUPPORT. A CLASS ACT ALSO REMEMBERS THAT MONUMENTALLY KIND ACTS DO NOT HAVE TO BE BIG PRODUCTIONS.

Part IX

DIFFICULT CONVERSATIONS AND
FAUX PAS RESCUES

CHAPTER 36

A Class Act Understands Tough Love

"Truth is tough. It will not break, like a bubble, at a touch; nay, you may kick it about all day like a football, and it will be round and full at evening."

—Oliver Wendell Holmes

Few situations test our civility and leadership qualities more than when we're forced to administer or receive tough love. It's gut-wrenching and soul-wrenching to deliver bad news to anyone or to be on the receiving end. Difficult messages regarding firings, layoffs, or even general reprimanding for unacceptable behavior place us in a business situation where we really need to know how to be and remain a Class Act.

DELIVERING BAD NEWS

The kindest way to convey bad news is to keep everything at the verbal level. If you are standing, stand up straight, hands at your sides. (Nobody said this would be comfortable.) Refrain from making any gestures. If you're sitting, keep your feet on the floor and your hands on the arms of the chair. Your tone of voice should be without judgment or emotion, almost as though you were saying, "it's raining outside."

Let the words carry your message when you're communicating something negative. We're adults, and we are often called upon to tell people things that will upset them. We cannot be responsible for someone liking or not liking that information. Still, we are 100 percent accountable for the way in which that information was delivered. The way in which we do this not only reflects our professional integrity but also reflects that of the company.

FIRING SOMEONE

Few things are more difficult than firing someone. Suppose you are dealing with an employee who has repeatedly missed work. The employee has been warned about it and all the appropriate documentation is in place. The proper way to fire someone would be to say something like this: "We've had this discussion three times in the past, yet, the agreed-upon changes haven't occurred. We're going to have to talk termination."

You might be thinking, "Wow, that's cold." But let's look at this from both the passive and aggressive stances. Picture someone about to terminate an employee. He shifts from foot to foot, glances about the room, fidgets, avoids eye contact. His face shows how bad he feels. Then he says, apologetically, "We've had this conversation three times in the past, yet the agreed-upon changes haven't occurred. We're going to have to talk termination. I'm so sorry."

Given that scenario, it's a good bet that the person in question truly doesn't believe he or she is going to be fired. And when they are fired, they will feel angry and betrayed. We must acknowledge that, in our own need to feel better about giving tough love, we often are more cruel to the receiver. This way, we are likely to send a mixed message, full of false hope.

On the aggressive end, it's even worse! Picture the terminator in a cocky position, hands on hips, using a snide tone of voice in saying, "We've had this discussion three times in the past. The word *termination* mean anything to you?" Sounds terrible, doesn't it? Yet it's easy to try to mask our own bad feelings in a cloak of seeming arrogance. Nothing could be less kind, less civil. Clearly, the first example is the best.

Whether we are terminating an employee or giving negative feedback to a colleague, the principles are the principles, and they work. It's important to be as direct as possible. Pain is unavoidable and small talk only prolongs discomfort, especially when both sides know what is about to happen.

Don't get into a long discussion about what might have been or what went wrong. Give one or two key reasons, and be sure to talk in terms of observable behavior.

Have at hand everything you need for the termination, including the final paycheck, severance pay, and relevant materials from the human-resources department, such as personnel forms and insurance and pension information. At the end of the meeting, recover security cards and keys, and company credit cards or purchase cards.

Don't drag out the departure. Get the terminated employee out of the office as soon as possible, or office morale might take a thumping with the ensuing gossip. If you can schedule the termination for a Friday, do so. That gives you the weekend to deal with any repercussions, and the terminated person gets some time to decompress. Then on Monday you can start the week fresh.

Be gracious. No matter what your personal differences were, shake the person's hand and wish him or her well. Thank them for the services they gave the company. Do not speak of this again, to anyone. Further remarks to anyone are inappropriate, like gossip, and should be avoided. Such conduct can only demean your respect and that of the employer. A Class Act knows this intuitively.

HANDLING OTHER UNCOMFORTABLE SITUATIONS

The following are typical situations you might encounter on a day-to-day basis. If handled with tact and class, any uncomfortable situation can be solved without insulting or demeaning anyone.

Boring Colleagues

Self-preservation is a good thing. So limit your time with boring people if you can.

Remember, though, that Class Acts make every effort to let other stars shine brightly. Take the cognitive approach and remind yourself that in the grand scheme of things, these few minutes will soon be history. Ask questions. Listen for the answers.

There's no need for self-punishment, however. When Barbara Boring tells you a story you've heard countless times, it's fair to say, "Oh, of course, now I remember how you. . . ." When you're in a group that's about to be told a story you've overdosed on, you can say, "I've heard this, so if you'll excuse me, I'm going to refresh my drink."

Be very careful to speak those words without rolling your eyes, sighing in frustration, or any other sign of irritation, frustration, or annoyance. Use the same unemotional tone of voice as you'd use to say, "It's raining outside." If you can't bring this off kindly, just hang in and bear the boredom.

Bad Table Manners

Dining skills are imperative in business. Sadly, no one will tell you that the reason they choose not to do business with you is that one of your representatives eats like a pig. You can't afford to allow the image of the company to suffer from your colleagues' or subordinates' shortcomings in this area.

You might ask your human resources department to deal with the lack of social skills, but I think the personal and direct approach is best. Remember the "it's raining outside" tone of voice, and take care not to sound condescending or arrogantly heavy-handed, not to mention self-righteous.

Praise the colleague's contributions to the company and say that, since he or she will be representing the company, it will be important to brush up on table manners and etiquette. Have an example of the objectionable behavior in mind, as specifics help us understand what behaviors need correcting. For example, "You might not be aware that you chew with your mouth open and it gets noisy." Or, "I noticed that you hold your fork like a cello and there's a better way to do it." Then provide a good etiquette book, such as my own *The Complete Idiot's Guide to Business Etiquette,* and remark on how valuable it is to have such a reference in one's personal library.

Colleagues Who Interrupt

Tread lightly and lightheartedly at first. You might wrap your comments in a compliment by saying something like, "Your energy and enthusiasm are strong points that I admire. You might not realize that you tend to interrupt me a lot. So I'm asking you to do your best to curb the habit and listen to what I say. Then I'd welcome your feedback and listen to you." This should work, but you might also want to work out a quiet signal regarding interruptions that is just between the two of you. Ask that it be used on you, as well.

Body Odors

This is a very sensitive, serious subject. In some cases, medical conditions and not poor hygiene cause bad breath and other odors. If it is a short-term problem, you risk more by saying something than by putting up with it. If a person has been ill, for example, there might not be anything he or she can do. In that case, nobody is more aware of the problem than the offender. When the problem is long-term, try to speak with someone in human resources and ask that the problem be addressed.

If you know someone who is friendly with this person, you might want to speak to him or her first and ask for counsel or, if you feel close enough to this person, you might say something like, "It's uncomfortable for me to say this to you. Still, I am your friend and want to make sure you don't sabotage yourself at work without even knowing it. Others have noticed that your body odor and/or breath are pretty strong. It's distracting and not doing you any good. Perhaps you can change the products you are using now. Once I used a deodorant for so long that it stopped being effective. That might be the case here. I've had success with Brand O and you might want to give it a try." Remember, your goal is to be helpful, not hurtful.

Gum Chewing

Tread lightly. That gum might be a stop-smoking tool. It's not fair to mandate a person's behavior in his or her own space unless lip smacking and gum popping become distracting. In that case, say something like, "You probably aren't aware of this, but I'm really distracted by the sounds of your gum chewing. I'd really appreciate it if you could do it more quietly." Chewing gum is a no-no at a business meeting. If you are the senior person at the meeting, it's perfectly appropriate to say, without judgment in your voice, "Let's get rid of the gum before the meeting."

HANDLING MORE SERIOUS ISSUES

Being true to yourself as a civil, successful, and centered person often means taking action when others are looking the other way. Here are some practical ways to handle some of the most difficult situations that arise.

Alcohol Abuse

The lovely dinner meeting with my colleague turned out to be a bad dream. Sure, we had wine with the meal. I loved every moment, morsel, and drop of it. Yet I was poorly prepared when she not only had wine, but slugged down cognac afterward, and commented that she had preceded our meeting with "a couple of Scotches."

I ended up taking her keys and checking her into the hotel that housed the restaurant where we dined. It all seemed like a dramatic hassle—and then I realized it wasn't over. I had to face this woman again. And what would I say when I did?

It can be a painful experience to watch an associate or friend behave badly after having one too many at a business function or the local watering hole.

So I turned to Todd Whitmer, senior executive officer of the Caron Foundation, a nationally recognized non-profit addiction treatment center, for advice on what to do to help a colleague avoid alcohol or drug-related career suicide—or worse.

Talk About How Their Actions Made You Feel

Whitmer says that work is one of the last places a drinking problem will surface, but friends and colleagues are likely to know a person is having a problem with alcohol before the boss does, and they can help steer him or her away from danger to self and career. These steps can help:

- If your friend could endanger herself, or others, intervene. Take the car keys, call a cab, or look her in the eye and ask her to leave with you.

- Wait until she is sober before you try talking to her. Be specific about what you observed, without accusing. For example, instead of, "You were really drunk last night," try, "I felt embarrassed about the joke you told last night. You don't ordinarily talk like that. Maybe you had too much to drink."

- Use "I" language; express your feelings such as alarm, fear, and sadness, not what you think is happening to the other person. "Although she may argue, she can't deny your feelings," Whitmer says.

- Express your concern and offer to provide feedback if you see the problem surfacing again. Talk to her before the next company gathering, and let her know you will signal when you sense inappropriate behavior coming on.

Offer Help, Not Counseling

Avoid the role of counselor. You can certainly show compassion and express your concern, but don't hesitate to say, "I'm not in a position to counsel you about what's going on."

You might say instead, "The last time all the managers went out for a drink after the strategic planning meeting, I was afraid, after the third drink, that your remarks about the boss were going to get you into trouble. I'm feeling some anxiety about tonight's business dinner. If I sense you're getting into dangerous territory, I'm going to give you that feedback. Does that make sense to you? When I say, 'Remember what we talked about yesterday?' that's the red flag."

If your company has an employee assistance program, steer your friend or colleague in that direction. If that resource is unavailable, contact an alcoholism information and treatment center to obtain useful information and give it to the concerned person. This is better than merely suggesting your friend make the contact and obtain the information about available help.

Drug Abuse

Most of us, at some point, will work with someone who is using illegal drugs. The numbers are scary. Seventy percent of drug users are employed full-time, and studies have show that almost eight percent of full-time workers report current drug use.

"Drug users keep their habit under cover at work because it's illegal and likely to get them fired," says Todd Whitmer. "So if you notice it, there's a good chance this person has been using for a while, and the addiction is pretty serious."

If you know a co-worker is using drugs, Whitmer advises taking steps to get the person into treatment, and has these suggestions:

- If personal safety is an issue, intervene. Do what is necessary to keep the person or others from harm, including taking him or her to the emergency room, calling the police or taking the car keys.

- Do not lie, make excuses, or try to cover up your friend's behavior. You need not say, "Jane is not in the meeting because she's snorting cocaine in the bathroom." You could say, "I'm not sure what's going on; I assumed Jane was coming to the meeting."

- Do not attempt to talk to colleagues about drug use while they are high. Wait until this person is coherent. Avoid accusations; be honest about your concerns without shaming or moralizing. Try something like, "I was really in a bad spot when they asked me why you missed the meeting. I am worried about what's happening to you. I would like you to get help. But I am not going to cover up for you if you're missing meetings, and I will not make excuses for you to others."

- Get help. Contact your employee assistance program. It provides assistance not only to employees but also to family members and others in the employee's life. If there is no program, call an addiction treatment center.

- If your colleague refuses help, you can collaborate with friends and family to confront the addict with his or her problem. Addiction treatment centers can connect you with a professional who can plan and guide a process called intervention.

A CLASS ACT WILL ALWAYS CONFRONT DIFFICULT SITUATIONS WITH UNDERSTANDING, COMPASSION, AND APPROPRIATE CONCERN.

CHAPTER 37

A Class Act Knows How to Use the Word "No"

"Suit the action to the word, the word to the action."
—William Shakespeare

"Just say no," the slogan reads. If only saying no were that easy . . .

When I was a very young child, my parents taught me to extend my hand and say, "Pleased to meet you." I learned how important it was, how kind it was, to make others feel comfortable and good about themselves. If only somebody had taught me then how to put on the brakes! Thus, I spent much of my life a raging people-pleaser, at considerable personal angst and expense.

All that wasted energy! I'd say "yes" to just about anybody. Heaven forbid we have a conflict. So as I spoke the words to assent, I'd be plotting my escape route, thinking something like, "Well, if I have a last-minute emergency, I can call this off with no hard feelings. Everybody understands emergencies. And for now, he or she will be pleased that I said "yes."

EASIER WITH THE FAMILY

With my family, I wasn't nearly so polite. I was quick to let them know of my great personal sacrifice. I said "yes" and accompanied it with sighs, rolling eyes, slow motion, tosses of my head, and enough obvious displeasure that

I figured nobody would ask me to do anything, ever again. But it never worked. More good energy down the drain.

On the rare occasions when I did say no, my explanations were so laborious and long that not only was I exhausted in the creating and telling, I'm certain that the person who had to listen to it was equally drained. Still more good energy down the drain.

What's wrong with this picture? I'll tell you. It's possible to disagree without being disagreeable, just as it's okay to say no. Just as we don't have to mean to be tough, being polite does not mean letting rude people have their way.

THE PRINCIPLES OF SAYING "NO"

The two principles that changed my life:

1. When you refuse to play the game, all the rules change.
2. Tell people what you can do; not what you can't do.

Here's how these principles work:

THE RULES OF NON-ENGAGEMENT

Let's say you're at a party and a "pusher"—that insistent, annoying individual who just knows you'd be better of with another drink, another dessert, another helping of mashed potatoes—accosts you. Or a colleague invites you to a Tupperware party her fourth cousin, once removed, is giving and drives home the point that you'd benefit so much from attending. You simply, firmly say, "No, thank you. I don't feel like dessert tonight." And, "Thanks, I have other plans that night." You don't play their game.

A key point is to remember to respond in as emotion-free a tone of voice as you would use if saying the phrase, "It's raining outside," so that when you decline you do not sound apologetic. The very minute you sound apologetic, they have their hooks in you, and you'll be stuck doing something you do not want to do.

If you do this, nobody can argue with you. It's your reality. So if you don't feel like having dessert, end of story—you do not owe anyone an explanation. Your "plans" could be watching your plants grow. So what? They are your plans.

You can use this same principle to deflect any irritating, intrusive, and offensive questions, such as, "How much money do you make?" My personal favorite response is, "If you'll forgive me for not answering that, I'll forgive you for asking it." The more faint of heart might do better with, "I can't imagine why you would ask me that," or "I simply do not discuss such personal matters. But thank you for your keen interest in them."

THE RULES FOR SAYING "NO" AT WORK

On the job, delivering the positive negative—or "tell 'em what you can do, not what you can't do"—is an essential skill for peaceful coexistence. It can get dicey if it's your boss making the unreasonable demands. Try responding with, "I'm glad to get the first half to you by three and the rest by noon tomorrow, if not before." You smile as you say this, and do not sound apologetic. (Remember to use the same tone as you would when saying, "It's raining outside.") Do not become defensive. People tend to get defensive when they know they're wrong.

Another useful approach is to lead the requester to your conclusion. That might sound like, "How did you learn to set your priorities and keep them when you came to this company? I really feel that I better concentrate on my own projects now, so I can give them the attention they deserve." Or, "Right now I'm in the middle of Project A. Would you like me to drop that now and pick up Project B for you?"

Suppose your colleague asks you to cover his or her telephone yet again this week. You say, "I understand that you're on full tilt, and I really can't pitch in now." Of course, expect persistence, because, after all, we are taught from childhood to be compliant and agreeable. You'll hear a litany of reasons why your immediate attention to his problem is essential. You say, "I understand, and I still cannot," or, "That's true, and I'm simply not able to do that." Thus, you are wearing down the wearer-down.

Here's a great tip. Don't use the word "but." "But" is what I call an "eraser word." The minute it leaves your lips, whatever you said before it is forgotten. So erase "but" from your vocabulary and replace it with "and."

When a Request Compromises Your Integrity

It's time to take a closer look at things when our integrity is compromised. We have three choices in any given situation.

1. Accept the situation.
2. Leave.
3. Change it.

The stakes get higher when our values and integrity are compromised. Your colleague asks you to fudge expense accounts, or violate a copyright. Say, "Sorry, I really can't do that" (again think, "It's raining outside"). Perhaps you can add something like, "Maybe you should reconsider the request. Do you realize the implications of what you asked?"

Usually changing a situation means changing ourselves in the way we react to things we do not like or do not want to participate in. Turning down a superior is, of course, risky. If you must do this, tell your supervisor that while you like your job/assignment in general, this particular thing makes you very uncomfortable. Although the conversation might sour your relationship completely (read: shoot the messenger), at least you will know you had the courage to stand by your ethics.

A CLASS ACT KNOWS HOW TO HANDLE DICEY SITUATIONS WITHOUT DISHONORING ANYONE.

CHAPTER 38

A Class Act Understands Cosmetic Procedures

"I was going to have cosmetic surgery until I noticed that the doctor's office was full of portraits by Picasso."

—Rita Rudner

AS THE CROW'S FEET FLY

"My God! What happened? Are you okay?"

The counterman of my neighborhood coffee shop was shocked by my appearance. I explained, as quietly as I could, that my "shiners" were the result of cosmetic surgery.

"You paid to have somebody to do that to you?"

I ordered my coffee to go. And went.

A DELAYED REACTION

Three days before, I'd had laser surgery to remove crow's feet from the edges of my eyes. Immediately afterward, I had checked myself out in the mirror. I looked no worse than if I'd applied a little too much "Cherries in the Snow" to my cheeks.

The next day, I went to lunch at a fancy restaurant. Nobody commented on my appearance.

At the end of the day, I paid a visit to my five-year-old nephew, Robert.

A look of puzzled concern replaced his usual sunny smile. "Aunt Mary, who did that to you?"

I told him the doctor had done it, because I wanted to look younger and gorgeous.

"Well, you don't," he informed me.

A five-year-old can say exactly what's on his mind. But one expects more diplomacy from an adult. Though my shiners have disappeared, the urge to dictate a few rules of thumb about the sensitive subject of commenting on someone's appearance has not.

SOME DO'S AND DON'TS

If you run into someone whose appearance is markedly different and you suspect cosmetic surgery, here are some suggestions of what you can do to keep the situation comfortable for all parties.

Don't blurt out a comment. Chances are that this person is undoubtedly feeling sensitive about their appearance anyway, so if you must ask, keep it to a simple question of concern and avoid any exaggerated reaction.

Don't ask. Even if you're dying to know, it's bad manners to ask if a person has had a "nose job" or "eye job." In fact, those terms should be avoided altogether. Again, if you must say something, try something like, "You look wonderful. Whatever you've been doing lately agrees with you." If this person wants you to know any details, leave it to him or her to tell you. (Remember this tactic also if you suspect someone is pregnant. There is no exchange more embarrassing than when one person says, "When is the baby due?" and the other responds, "There is no baby. I've just gained some weight.")

Don't criticize. If a person tells you he or she is contemplating cosmetic surgery, resist the temptation to call it a "crazy idea" and to try to talk the person out of it. It is equally important not to agree that the person does, indeed, need the work done. Respect the ability of others to decide for themselves, and honor their choices.

Don't judge. If a person tells you the cosmetic surgery has been done, the safest response is to ask if he or she is pleased with the results. Even if pressed, never judge the results. This is a classic "shoot the messenger" situation. The most diplomatic response, when the details of the surgery are shared, is to say, "I see what you mean, but only when you point it out."

Don't gossip. Never volunteer the names of others you know who have had cosmetic surgery. In fact, any gossiping about the subject is out of line. Any "cosmetic" procedure is, in fact, a medical procedure and therefore serious business.

Be solicitous. When people tell you they have had cosmetic surgery, ask how they're feeling, both physically and mentally. If you're the one who has had the surgery and you look markedly different, you can make it easier on those around you by opening the conversational door.

A Class Act knows that the subject of cosmetic surgery is a very personal issue and decision. If you notice that a person's appearance has changed, offer a compliment. Otherwise, keep mum. If you have decided to have "work done," it is up to you alone to discuss or not discuss the procedure.

BEING A CLASS ACT ALSO MEANS THAT YOU MAY HAVE TO BEAR THE BRUNT OF UNWANTED REMARKS FROM THOSE WHO ARE NOT CLASS ACTS.

Part X

DOING THE RIGHT THING

CHAPTER 39

A Class Act Knows How to Apologize Well

"Never apologize for showing feeling. When you do so, you apologize for the truth."

—Benjamin Disraeli

One of my most influential teachers said, "If you want to learn anything in this life; if you want to become the person God meant you to be, you must be willing to be wrong." He also is the guy who taught me that if I want to change anything, it means changing myself first. This means not copping out and blaming anyone or anything else when things don't go as they should—or more to the point, when they don't go my way.

OWN UP TO THE TRUTH

It's so easy to take somebody else's inventory and conclude that he or she is completely self-delusional. It's simple, yet not easy, to see that in ourselves.

Who wants to be wrong? Certainly not me. It seems, however, that I bungle things a lot. Big things and little things. But if I own up to causing the problem, don't blame it on anybody else or on circumstances, and apologize for whatever hurt feelings or losses I might have caused, whatever the magnitude of my errors, people are far more likely to forgive me.

It takes courage to apologize and mean it. When we apologize we are holding ourselves accountable to the truth. It also requires compassion to apologize. To do this, you need to put yourself in the other person's shoes and feel how they feel as a result of our misdeed. A true apology takes a bit of reflection; not just a knee-jerk "I'm sorry."

There is something sacred about apologizing. Especially when we realize that a true apology carries with it the appropriate amends. If we're not going to do something differently and thus heal the situation, our apology is dishonest. Apologies are sacred, because they help clear the path to moving forward in life after we've fallen and picked ourselves up again.

The companies we surveyed resented and wouldn't accept their suppliers blaming others for mistakes or refusing to get to the truth of matters. They would sooner discontinue the business relationship. In turn, companies were willing to stick with suppliers who were willing to take responsibility for their actions. Mistakes weren't unforgivable; lying about them was unacceptable.

In fact, sometimes the experience of "going to the fire" with a client or co-worker and making amends actually creates a stronger union.

THE MECHANICS OF APOLOGY

So you goofed. We all do. The question now is what are you going to do about it?

That, of course, depends on the magnitude of the goof. One thing is certain, you must say it in words and perhaps with flowers or some other gift.

Bless the immediacy of e-mail! Let's say you forget to return an important telephone call or you forget a lunch date. Maybe you kept somebody waiting a long while; maybe you failed to give proper public credit to someone. By all means, send an e-mail or telephone call right away—as soon as you've given some thought to what your slight must have meant to the receiver of it.

Still, an e-mail or a telephone call simply is not enough. Don't even think about apologizing by fax! This form is totally impersonal and rude in this circumstance. You will need to write a letter of apology.

Writing a Letter of Apology: The SSA Formula

SSA stands for SPECIFICITY, SIGNIFICANCE, ACTION. It is my foolproof SSA formula for writing letters of apology. This formula also works when composing letters of thanks, condolence, or congratulations. Write it on the best stationery you have and use a fountain pen, not ballpoint. Have it delivered by messenger or overnight courier. You might include an invitation to lunch—the ceremony of sharing food goes a long way to heal sore feelings.

First, admit that what you said or did was wrong and that you are truly sorry for having done it. Be specific. For example, "I am so sorry for having kept you waiting nearly an hour yesterday," is better than a bland, "I'm so sorry about yesterday."

Second, emphasize that there was no excuse for what you did, yet note any mitigating circumstances. Then acknowledge what your actions cost the other person in terms of time, energy, hurt feelings, etc. That's the significance. For example, "I could kick myself for not allowing enough time to navigate our fair city's streets. Especially since you were kind enough to make time for me when your plate already is overloaded with looming deadlines."

Third, say how you will make sure never to repeat your gaffe and mention whatever reasonable ideas come to mind for rectifying the damage you've caused. That's the action. For example, "I hope you know that I've learned a valuable lesson from this unfortunate incident. In the future, I will assume nightmare traffic conditions and allow time for them. Please let me take you to lunch next month to celebrate your making your deadlines. I will call you to make a plan. Meanwhile, I hope you will forgive my lack of foresight."

What an Apology Means

Remember to speak in terms of observable behavior and its effects. In other words, you can apologize for hurting someone's feelings with your sharp comments, but that doesn't necessarily mean that you are apologizing for what you think and feel. An apology does mean that you are repentant; that you will change your behavior and not repeat your slight.

When we were kids, our parents used to reproach us to "take things back" when we said something wrong. If only life were that easy.

Here is a classic example of this: When President Clinton was re-elected, television journalist David Brinkley commented when the election results were announced that he thought Clinton ran a boring campaign. In a nanosecond, the national media splashed, "Brinkley Calls Clinton a Bore." The following day, Brinkley apologized publicly to the president. He said that he deeply regretted making such a comment in a public forum and that he should have known better. He apologized for any bruised feelings or embarrassment he might have caused the president. Did he change his mind about the boring campaign? No way. In other words, he remained accountable for his thoughts, feelings, and behavior.

Clinton graciously accepted Brinkley's apology by saying that Brinkley's record over time was as a responsible, professional, and fair journalist and that one misguided comment could not displace that opinion of the newsman.

Accept apologies. Be gracious and sincere. Otherwise, you will undo the good in the experience. Obviously, if someone assassinates your character, steals your money and your spouse, this advice is not necessarily for you. Generally, though, authentically accepting someone's apology goes a long way toward forgiveness.

A CLASS ACT KNOWS THAT KNOWING HOW AND WHEN TO APOLO-GIZE IS INVALUABLE. IT RELIEVES STRESS, DIMINISHES RESENTMENT, AND PAVES THE PATH FOR PROGRESS.

CHAPTER 40

Epilogue: A Civil, Successful, and Centered Man

"If you want happiness for an hour, take a nap. If you want happiness for a day—go fishing. If you want happiness for a year—inherit a fortune. If you want happiness for a lifetime, help someone else."

—Chinese Proverb

In this final chapter, I will simply tell you about Clarence—my hero and Angel of Civility. Clarence reminds me, just by his daily example, of the inherent dignity of each and every human being. And in this world of pandemic rudeness, this is a very good thing.

FIRST IMPRESSIONS ASIDE . . .

Clarence's patrician voice and language put me off at first. Tall and silver-haired, with dancing blue eyes, he was pretty tough to miss at our neighborhood market and coffee shop. And he was compelling; I found myself listening to his every word.

Eventually, it dawned on me that I had never once heard a mean-spirited remark from this gentleman. In fact, he always had positive things to say, and—no wimp, he—said them with such delicious wit that after every encounter, I emerged a better person.

A RETIRED CORPORATE LAWYER, CLARENCE PAYS ATTENTION

Clarence is, by training, a corporate lawyer. His wisdom, experience, and erudition are genuine and vast. Now retired, he spends his days doing whatever he can, large or small, to better the lives of others. Things like:

- preparing a perfect pot roast for a weary friend

- painting this writer's office to bring "color and order" to the environment—"all the better for producing meaningful work"

- untangling a friend's nightmarish (and erroneous) five-figure bill from the phone company.

His Ivy League pedigree aside, Clarence just seems to know everything, including where to find the most intoxicating olive oil and how to build a gizmo to extract a long-dead mouse from behind a refrigerator. When I asked him how he knew so much, he replied, "I just pay attention."

He told me that the defining moment of his corporate life occurred when he was a high-profile lawyer in Washington, D.C., and heard Johns Hopkins University President Milton Eisenhower, younger brother of Ike, speak at a luncheon he gave for Hubert Humphrey, saying, "The greatest threat to our American way of life is not Communism or the Cold War, I believe. It is, rather, man's inhumanity to his fellow man."

AN INFECTIOUS LAUGH AND COMPASSIONATE HEART

Clarence brims with gusto and contagious laughter. And yet, he is compassionate and wise to the core. This is the man who consoled a bereaved friend, by saying, "Perhaps now it's up to us who are left to love one another a little bit more." And to me, at one downhearted moment: "Think about it. Don't worry about it."

When life's insanity and emotional chaos surround him, he finds intellectual refuge in books like David McCullough's biography of John Adams. Now there is a sane alternative to being on tilt!

A MAN OF ACTION

We all wring our hands and rant about the rudeness that seems to be eroding our lives: the cell-phone intrusions. The stolen taxicabs. The nasty salespeople. The littered sidewalks. The jaywalkers. People who don't show up for work on time, if at all. People who abuse themselves and others by blaming other people for their shortcomings. People who, by always putting themselves first, strain important relationships, even with people who love them.

But hasn't anyone noticed that if we want things to change, we must begin with ourselves? Haven't we learned that we learn best—and thus, teach best—by example?

That's why Clarence is an Angel of Civility. He doesn't preach it; he practices it—every day, in every interaction. He believes with every molecule of his being that every living thing deserves respect, and he gives it generously.

Clarence knows that a person's true worth is measured by the quality and integrity of his or her relationships. Our relationships are the most important components of our lives.

AN INSPIRATION

Good manners are based on the simple good deeds and words that spring from our hearts that nurture those relationships and keep them in repair.

Watching Clarence and others like him humbles and inspires me. I am grateful to be reminded that there are people in our midst who make our world a more civilized place—a better place.

When we look for Angels of Civility in our lives, we can and will find them. Better still, we can grow into such angels ourselves.

A CLASS ACT STRIVES TO BECOME AN ANGEL OF CIVILITY.

APPENDIX A

A CLASS ACT AND MEDITATION

Meditation and contemplation have been a part of my life for many years. Initially, I reached for this discipline when I was in great and painful need of focus, peace, and contentment, or to overcome specific obstacles. It was similar to flossing my teeth—only do it when there is a pressing need.

Disregarding my dentist's advice of regularity, I flossed when need was great.

Similarly, I used meditation for periodic solace, not as a regular life-enhancing practice.

I have grown to realize that daily meditation is an essential tool for a centered productive life.

THE SACRED GIFT

Einstein eloquently directed us to the fact that we all have two minds with which to work: the sacred gift of the intuitive, creative mind and the faithful servant of the logical, rational mind. It is the sacred gift's job to create an environment for the "5 Is" to show themselves; the faithful servant's job to act upon them.

THE "FIVE I's" ARE:

- Incubation

- Inspiration

- Intuition

- Illumination

- Insights

They are the suggestion of my coach, John Felitto, who advises that these five concepts flood our consciousness with positive possibilities and lighten our emotional state.

Since the sacred gift of the creative mind is more about being than doing, we cannot force it to do anything. Forcing causes stress and shuts down access to the "5 I's."

HUMAN BEING VS. HUMAN DOING

When we reflect on every area of our life, we grow closer to maintaining a healthy balance.

Set a time for contemplation. Felitto's 5 Is cover just about all areas of our life: health, career and finances, relationships, recreation, and contribution. Express gratitude and revisit successes. Create ideal outcomes. Surrender to the sacred gift and be alert for feedback. Take it with you. Take action.

The simple act of setting aside time to participate in the Five Is sends a powerful message to your subconscious and conscious mind that you are worthy and deserving of a wonderful life. My own sessions, in the morning and evening, take about twelve minutes. That's all.

Your contemplation can take the form of writing in a journal, deep breathing exercises, walking, listening to tapes. We are all different and learn differently. Experiment until you discover what's best for you.

The least effort and most fun are ingredients conducive to a "5 I" environment.

THE PROCESS

Begin by going to your favorite quiet place. Close your eyes and concentrate on your breathing as you take several deep breaths. This will help you relax, clear your mind, and prepare you for a dynamically focused state.

If you are more of a visual person, you might engage in visualization. If you have the need to touch, to feel, then you should do some writing. You might list all the things for which you are grateful and write down some self-created affirmations and their intentions.

If you are an auditory learner, you will evoke your intentions from within you and transform your thoughts into audible language. Your ears will hear your own voice and, in some cases, you will have your eyes involved by reading self-created intentions and notes aloud. This daily meditation has been so effective that I have included a transcript of my own tape at the end of this appendix.

Visit each of the five levels, first expressing gratitude and then reviewing past successes. This puts you on the success channel to stimulate and powerfully attract the 5 Is to your awareness.

First, there's your Health Level. Focus on what you are grateful for; consider your physical, mental, and spiritual health. For example, you might express gratitude that your have eyes and ears to appreciate the beauty of a wonderful day; the energy and vitality to enjoy being outdoors; feeling connected to the universe.

Then review your past successes: the fitness program you finally began, the attainment of an ideal weight, or overcoming an addiction problem. The idea is first to express thanks, then acknowledge yourself and how it feels when you're feeling good, feeling productive, feeling centered and effective.

Next, create ideal outcomes. Don't be afraid to think of big, magic-wand stuff. Let's say you are still in the ideal health moment. Stay in the present moment context. You are at your ideal weight, energized from your consistent fitness program; your mind is crystal clear, enjoying all of your realized goals and intentions. You are emotionally joyful and enthusiastic, yet peaceful. In creating ideal outcomes, pray as though you have already received them.

Now it's time to let it go, surrender it to your creative mind, and be alert for feedback. Trust that the feedback will come. You will have flashes of insight. You will find yourself saying things like, "It just dawned on me" or

"It came to me that I can do this or that." When these ideas come to you, allow your faithful servant to participate and help you take action. Honor your sacred gift by taking actions on insights that "come to you." In doing so, you express faith, attract more insights and begin to live the life you truly want.

PHYSICAL CHANGES BY AN UNWILLING YOGI

Just as I have yet to chant while meditating, I have yet to levitate in a yoga class or anywhere else, for that matter.

Frankly, the whole idea of yoga irritated me. It was so *slow*. It didn't *go* anywhere. Stretching was for wimps with too much time on their hands. BORING!

On our last summer vacation, a massage therapist told my husband, "Dan, I could work on your injured shoulder from now until Christmas and it wouldn't do you nearly so much good as a couple of yoga classes a week." Fortunately for both of us, Dan didn't say, "Great, start now, tell me when it's Christmas, and then we'll talk about yoga."

So we took our first yoga class together, under the tutelage of my friend, Maura Patrice, in Ojai, California. Maura and I have been friends for years, and I'd successfully avoided her classes all that time. While I knew that yoga was boring, Maura was anything but boring. And the same was true when I finally relented and took her class. She was downright funny. Humor somehow took the tension out of the stretching and helped us stretch that much further.

There is no competition in yoga. What a concept! How enormously liberating!

We relaxed and got into the moment. We weren't ashamed that it seemed like our hamstrings were the shortest known to humans. Or that suddenly we discovered muscles we never knew we had. What really mattered was that we felt great after the class.

So we went back for more, with just about any instructor we could find. Consistently, we felt great after class—more focused, more relaxed. Danny's chronic shoulder pain is history, and I have more mobility in my "typist's" neck than any massage, acupuncture, or chiropractic adjustment ever brought me.

Now both Danny and I do our best to make time for regular yoga classes.

Spiritual enlightenment? We're a ways from levitating, that's for sure. Yet back in Philadelphia, our teacher, Brie Neff, wisely advised us not to measure ourselves or our progress from class to class. Instead, she suggested recalling our first class, or where we were six months ago.

Neff pointed out that "if what you teach [manners] is based on respect for others, then the rules of my work [yoga] are based on respect for oneself. Like you, 'I teach what I want to learn.'"

At the beginning of my yoga practice, Maura Patrice commented, "Whenever I need to figure something out, whenever I know I must be honest with myself, I know I must get down on my mat." Puzzling comment then, it's beginning to make sense. Could enlightenment be in the offing? Who knows?

EXPERIMENT WITH YOUR OWN MEDITATION PROCESS

You might enjoy reading this transcript of the tape I used each day as I wrote this book. My friend, Barry Eisen, the Los Angeles-based consultant, actually made it for me. He combined his own relaxation and self-hypnosis techniques with my own affirmations. The affirmations reflect the 5 Is.

Go ahead and make your own audio tape. Your mind will respond to the sound of your own voice. I promise that if you commit to meditating twice a day for three weeks, you will notice positive changes in your judgment, thinking, focus, and demeanor. I guarantee that you will become far more centered than you are right now.

THE TEXT TO RELAX YOUR BODY AND MIND

All right, Mary, find a comfortably relaxed position and close your eyes.

Concentrate on the sound of my voice and let yourself relax. Become aware of your facial muscles; relax your eyes. Separate your teeth. If your jaw naturally drops down, let it do so. Allow your shoulders to become slack; feel the heaviness extending down your arms, stomach, and chest muscles.

Relax—more with every breath. Relax your body, relax your legs. Imagine that your physical body is drifting into a comforting sleep, yet you stay focused on the sound of my voice at all times, internalizing all positive and beneficial thought and suggestion.

Now take a comfortably deep breath in, holding it a moment, and as you exhale repeat inwardly, "One. I feel comfortable and deeply relaxed."

Now take a second breath, as you exhale it, repeat inwardly, "Two. I feel fine and wonderful."

Now take a third, comfortable breath in, as you exhale it, repeat inwardly, silently, meaningfully, "Three. I'm relaxing deeper than ever before."

As you now bring all of your attention to the bottoms of your feet, feel the tingling sensitivity of circulation turn to a powerful movement of relaxation, one that you may be able to see as well as feel moving through your toes, arches, insteps, and heels, as though from within a thousand fingers were massaging every muscle and nerve. This relaxation moves up from your ankles into the lower leg muscles and from within, imagine these muscles melting, dripping into shimmering pools of liquid there.

Continue this upward flow of relaxation through and around your knees and to the upper legs muscles, which release and relax like rubbery rubber bands, letting go completely. As you follow this flow of relaxation, moving it up through your hips and pelvic area into your lower back, imagine those lower back muscles unraveling and unwinding, becoming long and loose and limp.

This relaxation moves up your backbone into the middle portions of your back, where you allow it to touch, release, and relax muscles you didn't even know existed. Continue it even higher, through your upper back. See it, feel it moving higher through your shoulders and shoulder blades and deeply into those muscles that sometimes hold onto the tightness and the tensions of the weeks' activities.

Feel the shoulders slumping, feel the heaviness of muscles at rest, and from around your back through your sides into your stomach and chest, the front portion of your upper body relaxing more comfortably with each breath. And as you continue to relax, turning even deeper within, achieving a more dynamic, intuitive, and more creative and powerful state of being, and the deeper you allow yourself to relax, the more comfortable you allow yourself to become.

Now from the tops of your shoulders, extending down through your arms, like a massage moving through the upper arm muscles, follow it down through your elbows and to the forearm muscles. Bring it down through your wrists and around your fingers, where once again you may feel the tingle of circulation.

Using your creative and very powerful imagination, imagine now that all worries, tensions, anxieties, ill health, negativity, fear, stress, from whatever the source, are drifting from your mind, flowing gently down your shoulders and arms. Imagine them escaping through your fingertips and drifting into the nothingness from where they've come.

Imagine now that all self-imposed restrictions or limitations that serve no beneficial purpose are leaving you completely and drifting farther from you with each breath.

And relax your neck and throat. Completely relax. The breathing passageways become free and clear and open and this wave of relaxation continues up and over the back of your head, now moving throughout your scalp, down across facial muscles. Relax your eyes, and the muscles within your cheeks and lower jaw.

As relaxed as you are, or have ever consciously been, this is a plateau— a level of experience that you can go beyond, and the value in it is that you become more open, more responsive to your own positive suggestions. To achieve those levels already there, I'm going to count backward from ten to one. With each number's awareness, let yourself relax a little more deeply, so deep that by or at the count "one," you'll be two or three times more deeply relaxed than you are at this time, completely open to each positive and beneficial thought and suggestion.

THE COUNTDOWN

Imagine the number "ten." With it, feel your arms and legs growing heavier and heavier as muscles continue to release and relax.

"Nine." Go deeper and more inward with each breath.

"Eight." All outside noises, sounds, distractions, even the chatter from inside you will serve to focus and relax you even more.

"Seven." Letting go of any resistance from within, moving through and beyond that.

"Six." Feeling very much at peace.

And "Five." Going deeper.

And "Four." All physical discomforts, disorders that serve no beneficial purpose are leaving you completely.

"Three." Deeper still.

"Two." So comfortable. Going even deeper now with a comfortable breath.

"One."

Messages to Myself

Still focusing on the sound of my voice. Internalizing only positive and beneficial thought and suggestion. You have ultimate trust, faith, and confidence in yourself and your capabilities. You begin each day with a positive energy that moves through everything that you do. When you fall asleep, at the appropriate time, you fall asleep quickly, sleep thoroughly and deeply, and wake up fully refreshed at your designated time, looking forward to each day with great anticipation and enthusiasm.

VISITING MY HEALTH LEVEL: THE FAB FIVE

You are in excellent health, which literally gets better every day, as all of your systems work in harmony for this excellence. See yourself covered and filled with this white healing light moving through every cell and fiber within you.

You support this throughout the day by making wise physical choices of exercise and food, and putting your mind where it literally will attract all of the very best.

NOW I GRATEFULLY VISIT MY CAREER LEVEL

You're in the process of attracting all that you need to. Everything that you need to do, to know, to have, you will attract and allow your ideal writing experience to manifest. You love knowing that you're serving thousands and even millions of people through your work in print, the Internet, and TV.

You love knowing that your supreme good health and ideal weight make you effective and compelling. You love knowing that with complete joy you enjoy your ideal energy, health, and weight, making you the best channel for the highest good. You love knowing how it feels doing the work that you love. You appreciate this more each day.

You love knowing that you've written a syndicated column for ten years, a great source of satisfaction.

You love knowing that you have published five very successful and profitable books that have affected peoples' lives in the most positive of ways.

You love knowing that you created "Ms. Demeanor."

NOW I CELEBRATE RELATIONSHIPS

You love knowing that you have attracted the support and loyalty of Letitia Baldrige, your hero, and that she entrusts you to carry on her work. You feel privileged in the association.

You love being married to Danny, your best friend, lover, and cheerleader. You love knowing that your marriage grows closer and more invincible with every breath that you take.

You love knowing that the spirit within is joyously aligning you to serve the highest good.

You love knowing how it feels when all the right, perfect things fall into place.

Affirming My Goals

You love knowing that your unconscious mind will easily recall and remember everything that you need to know during the process of crafting your book.

Your physical environment while writing your book is peaceful, calm, and comfortable. Your writing flows to you quicker than ever, and ideas and concepts gel quickly and easily.

Barry Eisen's Tip For Peak Performance

In this regard, on either hand I'd like you to circle the thumb and the index fingers, gently touching these two fingers together.

As you engage in the creative process, or problem solving, or literally any activity that requires excellence, or excellent focus and concentration, you remember a technique that we refer to as "waking hypnosis" for peak performance on demand. At those times of invention, participation, you'll circle those same two fingers as they are now circled. At those times, with your eyes opened or closed, you'll take one or two comfortable breaths and tell yourself, silently, internally, how you're going to perform in the upcoming activity. You will then uncircle the fingers and then deal with the activity, whether it be personal or business, whether it takes seconds, minutes, or hours, you will find yourself ultimately focused, better concentrated than ever before, as you use this anchoring, this little trigger mechanism known as waking hypnosis numerous times each day with great excellence.

You may uncircle your fingers.

THE WRAP-UP

You love how your supreme eagerness is attracting all the right next steps. All the right, perfect people are coming to you, from known and unknown sources. You're attracting them like a powerful magnet attracts metal.

You love how it feels finishing each section of the book and being in total gratitude for the process, as you release all of the details to the spirit within.

And so it is each time that you listen to this session, you become more open and more responsive to each positive thought, constantly showing yourself what you can do, rather than what you can't.

Now, at the conclusion of this session, either allow yourself to drift into a comforting sleep, or count up from one to six, and when you open your eyes, experience great energy. Either go to sleep or count up now.

VOILÀ!

This entire process takes twelve minutes. You probably noticed that I used language that recalled good feelings. Just remembering those good feelings lightens my emotions and raises my energy level. It helps solve problems, just by removing myself from them.

Index

accountability, virtue of, 11–13
afternoon tea, 175
alcohol. *See also* cocktail parties; drinking; drinks
    abuse, 236–37
    bar-hopping and, 152
    declining, 168, 181, 194, 209
    substitutes for, 103
    two-drink limit for, 194
America, rudeness in, 27–29
anatomy
    of conversationalist, 65–66
    of restaurant, 188–89
Angel of Civility, 253–55
apology(ies), 249
    accepting, 251
    letter of (SSA formula), 250–51
    meaning of, 250–51
    mechanics of, 250–52
    as sacred, 250
appearance, importance of, 108
attire. *See* clothing
audience members, responsibilities of, 97–98

bad breath, 235
bad news, delivering, 231–32
bad service, 28

bad table manners, 234
Bailey, F. Lee, 143
balance, work-life, 139
Baldrige, Letitia, 115, 144–45, 265
bar/bat mitzvahs, 220
bartender, 188–89
    tipping of, 129
bellman, tipping of, 128
Benson, Herbert, 38–39
bereavement. *See* condolence
birth celebrations, 220
black tie, 111–12
"bobble-head," 142
body language, 51, 52, 63
body odors, 235
boring colleagues, 233–34
boss
    bullying, 13
    celebrations and, 219, 220
    dinner with, 103, 184–85
    gifts to, 122
    how to treat, 138
    private club of, 214
boundaries, 18
bread, 164
breathing, 9, 37
    belly, 9, 39, 96–97
bridal shower celebrations, 219
Bridget Jones' Diary, 116

Brinkley, David, 252
buffet meal. *See* meal, buffet
bullying boss, 13
business casual clothes, 113–14
business entertaining
    at home, 192, 199–205
    in private clubs, 212–14
    in restaurants, 184-189, 206–11
business etiquette, 136–38
business meal. *See* meal, business
business mistakes, ten most common,
    29–33
busser, restaurant, 189

call waiting, 79–80
calling cards, 93–94
captain, restaurant, 188, 211
car, as "branch office," 158–59
Caron Foundation, 236
caterers, 201, 202
celebrations, 217–21
    bar/bat mitzvahs, 220
    birth, 220
    boss and, 219, 220
    bridal shower, 219
    christening, 220
    engagement, 219
    gifts v. cards for, 218
    retirement, 220–21
    wedding, 219
cell phones, 28, 80–81, 97, 106, 166
    in cars, 82
    rules, 81–82
Chaplin, William F., 56
chef, 188
children
    becoming successful adults, 3–4
    conduct of, 28
christening celebrations, 220
civility
    angel of, 253–55
    in business events, 135–40

at dinners and tea, 171–78
in meetings, 141–46
in office relationships, 147–53
in restaurant entertaining, 206–11
at table, 163–70
class act, qualities of, 3, 5–6
Clinton, William, 252
clothing, 108–16
    appropriate, 8–9
    black tie, 111–12
    business casual, 113–14
    fit of, 110
    gym, 106
    inappropriate, 32
    informal, 112
    quality of, 111
    semi-formal, 112
    summer style, 114–16
    for teleconferencing, 82–83
    wardrobe for men, 113
    wardrobe for women, 112–13
    white tie, 111
club personnel, tipping of, 130–31
coat-check person, tipping of, 129
cocktail parties, 179, 193–95
communication
    body language, 51, 52
    effective, 49–54
    listening skills, 51–53, 62–64
    negative feedback, 53–54
    perception in, 50
    telephone, 30
complaint handling, 69–70
compliment giving, 64
concierge, tipping of, 129
condolence, 226–27
    etiquette, 222–23
    what to say as, 224–26
confidence, building of, 7–10
conflict resolution, 69
contributions, giving, 120–22
conversation(s), 61–68
    changing subject of, 66

first impressions in, 61–63
listening during, 62–64
personal information in, 66
questions never to ask in, 67–68
silence during, 66
small talk in, 61, 63
starting, 64–65
conversationalist, anatomy of, 65–66
Copeland, Charles, 63
copyright protection, 89
corporate governance, 22–23, 25
results of bad, 23–25
corporations, responsibilities of, 22–26
correspondence
cards, 93
handwritten letters of apology as, 250–51
handwritten letters v. e-mail in, 91–93
stationery, 92–94, 157, 158
cosmetic surgery
"do's and don'ts" of, 244–45
reaction to, 243–44
courtesy, common, 27–28
Crane & Company, 92–93
crises, handling, 4–5
criticism
constructive, 31, 53–54
public, 31, 70
cutlery, 163, 172
cyberspace, 85–90

Dalton, Jane, 19
dating at work, 147–53
corporate policies on, 147–48
"don'ts" of, 151–53
getting caught, 153
guidelines for, 151
initiating, 149
not flaunting, 148–49
superiors dating subordinates in, 150

death. See condolence
delivery service, tipping of, 131
dentist, importance of, 9
dieting in restaurants, 103–4
dining
bad table manners in, 234
demeanor during, 167–68
for health, 102
tricky foods in, 168–69
dining etiquette, 163, 166–67
appearance in, 164
bread in, 164
chewing in, 164
cutlery in, 163
handbags/briefcases in, 166
lipstick in, 165
napkins in, 164
smoking in, 165
speed in, 165
teeth picking in, 165
dinner, with boss, 103, 184–85
disagreements, 69–74, 71–73
avoiding public, 70
fair-fighting tips for, 71–73
proceeding with, 70
tone of voice during, 70
dishwasher, restaurant, 189
doorman, tipping of, 128, 129, 130
"Dr. Julia," 101–2
dress. See clothing
dress codes, 32, 115
drinking. See also alcohol; cocktail parties
bar hopping and, 152
declining alcohol in, 168, 181, 194, 209
parties and, 103
drinks, 194–96
limit for, 194
meeting for, 193
restaurant entertaining for, 208–9
drug abuse, 237–38
dry cleaners, 9

Einstein, Albert, 43, 257
Eisen, Barry, 39, 261, 265–66
Eisenhower, Milton, 254
Elizabeth II (queen of England), 108
e-mail
    addressing, 86
    apologies, 250
    copyright issues, 89
    flaming, 87
    flawed medium of, 85
    formatting, 86–87
    handwritten notes/letters v., 91–92
    hoaxes, 87–88
    netiquette, 85–86
    passwords, 88–89
    security, 88
    spam, 88
engagement celebrations, 219
engineer, tipping of, 128–29
Enron, 11, 22
entertaining. See home, entertaining
    at; private club, entertaining at;
    restaurants, entertaining in
entrepreneurial businesses, 157–58
etiquette
    business, 136–38
    condolence, 222–27
    dining, 163–70
    exercise class, 106
    exercise pathway, 105
    manners v., 136
    netiquette, 85–86
    private club, 212
    rules of, 4
    telephone, 84
exercise, 8, 103, 104
exercise class etiquette, 106
exercise path etiquette, 105
eye contact, 53, 56

facial, tipping for, 130
Faigus, Marty, 19

fair-fighting tips, 71–73
"faithful servant," 39, 41, 43, 257,
    259–60
Farel, Julien, 117
fashion judgments, 109
fast-food servers, tipping of, 130
Felitto, John, 258
Fiddler on the Roof, 217
firing someone, 232–33
first impressions, 61–63
"5 Is," 257–60, 261
"Five P's," 143, 180
food delivery people, tipping of, 130
foods, tricky, 168–70
forgiveness, virtue of, 13–14
formal meal. See meal, formal

garage staff, tipping of, 129, 130
gifts
    for boss, 122
    bought online, 122–23
    v. cards, 218
    gift certificates as, 123
    ideas for, 124–25
    questions for giving, 124
    recycling, 123
    workplace, 122
giving, 10, 120–11
Global Crossing, 22
gloves, 57, 166
Good Morning, America, 3–4
gossip, 18–21, 20–21, 148, 152
Grant, Hugh, 116
gratuities. See tipping
grooming, 8–9, 117–19
guest list, making of, 202–3
gum chewing, 235
gym
    clothing, 106
    guidelines, 106–7
    locker-room diplomacy in, 107

hair, professional-looking, 117–19
hair stylist, tipping of, 130
handshakes, 56–57
handwritten letters
    of apology, 250–51
    v. e-mail, 91–93
headwaiter, 188, 211
health, 8, 101–7
    dining out for, 102–4
    exercise paths for, 105
    party smart for, 102–3
    self respect from, 102
    working out for, 104
high tea, 176
home, entertaining at, 199–205
    caterer for, 200, 202
    fear of, 200
    formal dinner as, 201
    guest list for, 202–3
    guest of honor in, 201, 204
    informal dinner for, 201
    late guests in, 204
    reciprocity in, 205
    seating logic for, 203–4
    starting small, 200
    unexpected guests in, 204–5
home, working from, 154–59
    car as "branch office" for, 158–59
    childcare help for, 156
    exercise and, 156–57
    familial concerns of, 155
    personal issues in, 154–55
    resolving conflicts in, 156
    schedules for, 155, 158–59
    starting your business, 157–58
host/hostess, restaurant, 188
hosting
    business social event, 182–83
    at home, 199–205
    at private club, 212–14
    in restaurants, 184–89, 206–11
Hotel Bel Air, 118
housekeeper, tipping of, 129

human being v. human doing, 258
Humphrey, Hubert, 254
hypnosis, 38, 39
    walking, 265–66

"I" language, 71
informal attire, 112
informal dinner at home, 201
integrity, 242
Internet, web surfing, 89–90
interrupting, 52, 72
    colleagues, 234–35
introductions, 55–59
    mechanics of, 55–57
    names in, 58–59
    rank in, 57–58
    value of, 32
invitations, 31
    reciprocity in, 205
    for restaurant entertaining, 207

J.E. Caldwell & Co., 92, 94
Johns Hopkins University, 254

Lammers, Thea, 41
language, vulgar, 28, 31–32
Lara, Antoinette, 118
letters
    of apology (SSA formula), 250–51
    handwritten, 91–93
lipstick, 165
listening, 51–53, 62–64
locker-room diplomacy, 107
"lounge lizard," 142

Machiavellian manners, 31
maitre d', 188–89, 207, 208
    tipping of, 130
make-up, 116

manicure, tipping for, 130
manners
    bad table, 234
    business meal, 185–86
    v. etiquette, 136
    good, 255
    Machiavellian, 31
massage, tipping for, 130
McCullough, David, 254
meal, buffet, 176–77
    tipping at, 129
meal, business, 184–85
    control of, 186–87
    hosting, 187–88
    manners, 185–86
    restaurant staff during, 188–89
meal, formal, 171
    arrival at, 171
    courses during, 174–75
    at home, 201
    place setting for, 172–73
    toasting tips for, 174
    wine service during, 173
meditation, 38–42, 257–66
    daily, 257, 259–60, 261–66
    "5 Is" for, 257–60, 261
    peak performance from, 265–66
    process, 259–60
    tape transcript, 261–66
    visualization v., 39
    visualizing public speaking
        through, 96–97
meetings, 141–46
    bad reputation of, 141
    Baldrige, Letitia on, 144–45
    cast of characters in, 142–43
    guidelines for, 145–46
    preparing for, 143
    rehearsing, 146
meetings and greetings, 55–56
Mengers, Patti, 199
message-taking, 30
mistakes to avoid, in business, 29–33

Mitchell Organization, The, 29
mobile phones. See cell phones
Ms. Demeanor (newspaper column), 15,
    265

names
    correct use of, 31
    in introductions, 58–59
    remembering, 59
napkins, 164, 172
Neff, Brie, 261
negative attitudes, 29–30
negative feedback, 53–54
netiquette, 85–86
New York Times, 141
"no," saying, 239–42
noblesse oblige, 22, 23, 24, 25
note taking, as listening skill, 53
notes, handwritten, 92–93

observable behavior, 54
observable fact, 54
office parties, 151
"on tilt," 37, 254
online shopping, 122–23
open-ended questions, 64

parents, responsibility of, 28
parking attendant, tipping of, 129
parties, office, 151
Patrice, Maura, 260, 261
PDA's (public displays of affection),
    152–53
peace, 37
peak performance, 265–66
pedicure, tipping for, 130
personal issues, resolving, 140
personal trainer, tipping of, 130
phones. See cell phones; telephones
plastic surgery. See cosmetic surgery

prayer, a collective, 44–45
priorities, refocusing, 139
private club, entertaining at, 212–13
    boss's club for, 214
    dress code in, 213
    tipping policy in, 213–14
profanity, 28, 31–32
Public Agenda Foundation, 27–29
public criticism, 70
public speaking
    audience responsibilities during,
    97–98
    fear of, 95–97
    Toastmasters International for,
    95–96
    visualization for, 96–97
"pundit," 143

questions
    how to ask, 73
    never
        to ask, 67–68

raise, asking for, 139
receiving, 10
reciprocity in invitations, 205
Relaxation Response, The (Benson),
    38–39
restaurant staff, 188–89. *See also* spe-
    cific restaurant staff
restaurants, entertaining in, 206–11
    business talk during, 210
    choosing a restaurant for, 206
    dress rehearsal for, 207–8
    drinks during, 208–9
    hosting and, 184–88, 208
    invitations for, 207
    ordering dinner during, 209
    seating order for, 208
    selecting wine when, 209–10
    tipping after, 129–30, 210–11
rest-room attendant, tipping of, 129

retirement celebrations, 220–21
Robert's Rules of Order, 146
romance, office, 147–53
room service, tipping for, 128
Roosevelt, Eleanor, 5
RSVP, 31, 180
rudeness, 27–33
*Rules of Civility and Decent Behavior In
    Company and Conversation* (Wash-
    ington), 21
rumors. *See* gossip
run-around, the, 32–33

"sacred gift," 39, 41, 43, 257, 259–60
saying "no," 239–42
secrets, 17–18
Seinfeld, Jerry, 95
self-confidence, 7–10
self-discipline, 9
self-hypnosis. *See* hypnosis
semi-formal attire, 112
September 11, 29
server, restaurant, 188–89
    tipping of, 129
service v. servitude, 126–27
sexual harassment, 149
Shakespeare, William, 239
shoemakers, 9
shoes
    men's, 113
    summer, 115
    women's, 112
silence, 52
Silva Method, 41
small talk, 61, 63
smiles, 51, 56, 115
smoking, 165, 182
social clubs, 212–13
social events, business, 180
    circulating at, 182
    good guest at, 180–82
    hosting, 182–83

Society of Professional Journalists, 199

sommelier, 189, 211

speaker phones, 79–80

sportsmanship, 104

SSA formula, for letter of apology, 250–51

stage fright, 96–97

stationery, 92–93
  calling cards, 93
  correspondence cards, 93
  home office, 157, 158
  wardrobes, 93–94

stress, 37, 40

Stress Directions, 40

summer style clothes, 114–16

table manners, bad, 234

tailors, 9, 110

taxi driver, tipping of, 129

tea
  afternoon, 175
  high, 175–76

technical support, tipping of, 128–29

telecommuting. *See* home, working from

teleconferencing, 82–84

telephone(s), 30, 75–84. *See also* cell phones
  call waiting on, 79–80
  etiquette, 84
  mistakes to avoid, 74–77
  phone tag and, 79
  speaker phones on, 79–80
  teleconferencing, 82–84
  voice mail on, 77–79

Ten Commandments
  of Exercise Path Etiquette, 105
  of Responsible Business Behavior, 15–16

termination, 232–33

thank you, saying, 121

Thoresen, Carl, 14

tipping. *See also* specific jobs and serv-ices
  generosity in, 127–28
  holiday, 130–31
  hotels, 128–29
  personal service, 130
  private club, 213–14
  restaurant, 129–30, 210–11
  salon, 130

tithing, 121–22

titles, correct use of, 31

toasting tips, 174

Toastmasters International, 95–96

tough love, 231, 232

Tournier, Paul, 17

Training (magazine), 113

trust, 11–12, 18

Trust and Betrayal in the Workplace (Reina & Reina), 12–13

trustworthiness
  determining your own, 12–13
  virtue of, 17–21

Twain, Mark, 95, 222

uncomfortable situations, handling, 233–38

University of Alabama (study), 56

valet, tipping of, 128

virtue of
  accountability, 11–13
  forgiveness, 13–14
  trustworthiness, 17–21

visualization, 38, 39, 40–42

voice mail, 77–79

waiting, 30

walking hypnosis, 265–66

Wall Street Journal Guide to Wine, 192

wardrobe
  for men, 113

stationery, 93–94
    for women, 112–13
Washington, George, 21
web surfing, 89–90
wedding celebrations, 219
Weiss, Janet, 94
white tie, 111
Whitmer, Todd, 236–38
Wilde, Oscar, 163, 193
Windows on the World Complete Wine Course, 192
wine
    approving, 191
    choosing, 190–91
    glasses, 166, 173, 192

at home, 192
    learning about, 192
    sommelier/steward, 129, 189, 211
"wise guy," 142
Woods, Tiger, 38, 136
working from home. *See* home, working from
working out. *See also* exercise
    in groups, 104
    sportsmanship in, 104
writing advice, 94

Yale University (study), 117
yoga, 260–61

About the Author

Mary Mitchell brings civility to life.

Ms. Mitchell established The Mitchell Organization in 1989 as a locus for her growing professional activities as columnist, author, speaker, trainer, consultant, and coach. She is renowned for removing the starch from etiquette, a subject often perceived to be stuffy.

More than fifty major corporate clients have learned and profited from Ms. Mitchell's cogent observation, "Your company's competitive advantage is directly related to the social and communications skills of its employees."

As such, her work in the areas of customer and client services has met with acclaim from leading multinational service organizations, especially in the legal, accounting, and hospitality industries.

Ms. Mitchell's books have been translated into Japanese, Chinese, Korean, Spanish, and Bulgarian.

She is an avid athlete and lives in Philadelphia with her husband.

Ms. Mitchell is reachable at mary@themitchell.org.